What SUCCESSFUL
Teachers Do in
Inclusive Classrooms

What **SUCCESSFUL** Teachers Do in Inclusive Classrooms

60 Research-Based Teaching Strategies That Help Special Learners Succeed

Sarah J. McNary ◉ Neal A. Glasgow ◉ Cathy D. Hicks

CORWIN PRESS
A Sage Publications Company
Thousand Oaks, California

KH

For information:

Corwin Press
A Sage Publications Company
2455 Teller Road
Thousand Oaks, California 91320
www.corwinpress.com

Sage Publications Ltd.
1 Oliver's Yard
55 City Road
London EC1Y 1SP
United Kingdom

Sage Publications India Pvt. Ltd.
B-42, Panchsheel Enclave
Post Box 4109
New Delhi 110 017 India

Printed in the United States of America

Library of Congress Cataloging-in-Publication Data

McNary, Sarah J., 1967-
What successful teachers do in inclusive classrooms : 60 research-based teaching strategies that help special learners succeed / Sarah J. McNary, Neal A. Glasgow, and Cathy D. Hicks.
    p. cm.
Includes bibliographical references and index.
ISBN 1-4129-0628-8 (cloth) — ISBN 1-4129-0629-6 (pbk.)
    1. Inclusive education. 2. Effective teaching. 3. Classroom management.
I. Glasgow, Neal A. II. Hicks, Cathy D. III. Title.
LC1200.M36 2005
371.9′046—dc22

2004027694

This book is printed on acid-free paper.

06 07 08 09 10 9 8 7 6 5 4 3 2

Acquisitions Editor:	Faye Zucker
Editorial Assistant:	Gem Rabanera
Production Editor:	Kristen Gibson
Copy Editor:	Diana Breti
Typesetter:	C&M Digitals (P) Ltd.
Indexer:	Sheila Bodell
Proofreader:	Penelope Sippel
Cover Designer:	Michael Dubowe

2/7/08

Contents

Foreword

What is the magic formula to help special learners succeed? Where is the magic bag of tricks that every special education teacher seems to have in order to help "those" special kids learn? I know I would be a more effective general education teacher in teaching "those" special learners in my classroom if I knew the magic techniques and formula . . . if I had the magic bag of tricks!

This is the sentiment described time and time again by almost every general education teacher, from the brand new teacher to the seasoned veteran. Most general education teachers are unfamiliar with effective strategies and techniques employed to teach special learners. In fact, the unfamiliarity can go beyond a lack of knowledge—a real sense of fear can set in. General education teachers often feel a sense of hopelessness and fear due to limited knowledge of special learner issues and needs, and they may not know how to even begin to approach the academic needs of the student.

Through my 10 years experience as the Director of Pupil Personnel Services in the San Dieguito Union High School District, 12 years experience as a college instructor, 16 years teaching experience in the K–12 public schools, and 8 years as a commissioner with the California Commission on Teacher Credentialing, I confidently state the fact, "teachers strive to teach all learners."

The reader about to embark on this book is in for a real dose of magic! The 60 research-based strategies to help special learners succeed are presented in a clear, concise reference format including "real life" teaching application techniques for today's challenging classroom.

Real teachers use these strategies and techniques in their classrooms. Although the strategies are research based, the real testimony comes from the experienced teachers and authors of this book. Their knowledge and teaching experience is moving and compelling. Still not convinced of the magic? Head to North San Diego County to the San Dieguito Union High

School District to see for yourself! Treat yourself to a visit to observe the authors Sarah McNary, Neal Glasgow, and Cathy Hicks in action in their classrooms. Believe me, you will not only be convinced, but you will want to thank me personally. We are grateful they elected to share their knowledge, teaching experiences, and promising practices with their readers.

This book is about all students learning. The strategies are designed to guide the teacher through the process of adapting the teaching practices and learning environment to address the needs of all learners. The instructional strategies presented are relevant for any student, any grade level.

Special learners deserve the chance to be taught in the general education classroom with effective strategies necessary for individual student success. General education teachers deserve the knowledge of the research-based instructional strategies paired with hands-on application techniques.

Yes, you deserve the magic in this book! So here it is—the magical techniques to help students. Keep it on your desk within reach at all times. Enjoy learning and teaching. Most of all, enjoy and celebrate your students' success!

Torrie Norton

Preface

Sarah McNary recalls: My first full-time teaching contract began in October 1991. I was following a parade of substitute teachers into a highly unruly and disorganized home economics classroom. Gradually order returned and I was able to focus my energies on quality lesson planning.

Using district guidelines as well as the objectives developed by the local community college that partnered with my program, I created a broad meal plan overview course that focused on budget and nutrition. I was proud of my curriculum and the class seemed to be running smoothly with the exception of one group of students who was just not "getting it."

In those days, special education students had most of their classes with special education teachers and then would "mainstream" for an elective and PE. My foods class was an obvious choice because "everyone needs to eat." At my inner city high school with over 2,500 students, I had 11 to 13 students with special needs in every class—several with severe handicaps. I found myself questioning my "one size fits all" approach to instruction as I realized that some of my students simply could not complete the lessons as I had designed them.

More and more, my thoughts returned to those students and I began to experiment with alternative assignments that would still convey the objectives of the lesson while being achievable for these students.

I asked myself, "How can a student on crutches stand at the stove to make stir-fry?" In that low-income school there were no special stands, stools, or adaptive equipment, but the staff room did have a hotplate to lend.

As the year progressed, I found myself drawn more and more to this population. It became a challenge to puzzle out the possibilities to arrange everything so that learning could take place. I knew that I was making a difference and it was addictive. The following summer I accepted another full-time contract—this time teaching a special day class at the middle school. I was hooked!

Later, I became a resource specialist, and although special education has changed substantially over the years, the one thing that hasn't is the concern that it brings out in general education teachers. Many teachers have expressed their worry, dismay, and sometimes anger at the number of students with special needs they find in their classes. Whether the students have difficulties with language, reading delays, or behavior, the teachers' concern continues. After listening to their complaints, I began to hear a common thread. These capable and concerned teachers were sharing a common emotion—fear. After priding themselves on being excellent and dedicated teachers, the fear of having students who might not learn was overwhelming. I believe that given the right tools and strategies, almost any teacher can provide a positive learning environment for almost every student.

As I began to work with these teachers, I realized that they needed validation (yes, it is more challenging to teach diverse learners), concrete suggestions for effective instruction (practical tips to use today, not theory and philosophy), and time to practice these ideas (support over a period of time using a reflective model that allows the students to give feedback in addition to the teachers' ongoing reflective practice).

In today's world of IDEA (Individuals with Disabilities Education Act) mandating the "Least Restrictive Environment" and No Child Left Behind which requires that highly qualified and credentialed teachers deliver instruction to students, more and more students with disabilities will be receiving instruction in general education classrooms. There is ample research out there, but where do we go to find out what works and what doesn't? Unlike many other professions, primary literature generated from educational research, experimentation, and investigation is usually a world away from the day-to-day grind of the classroom teacher. Rarely does that type of information filter into a teacher's professional life or development. Yet it is there. People conduct research on how teachers teach, how students with special needs learn, and how all stakeholders in the educational environment influence each other in the process. Yes, there are others out there concerned about the quality of the instructional experience for those students who don't fall into the average range.

For us, "research" is defined as the final product of a scientific investigation of measurable and observable phenomena. This concept of research differs from a person's anecdotal feeling, thoughts, opinions, and beliefs. Research results and conclusions supported by real data help define what works and what doesn't. This information can make us all better at what we do. Research literature is selected based on a journal's or article's validity and its ability to connect us, in new more useful ways, to authentic classroom situations and the common problems teachers routinely face in their professional environments. If it is good, we condense the knowledge contained in the literature and share it, much like all of us freely share our knowledge with our everyday colleagues. We write about the research in the same way we would verbally share it in the school lunch- or workroom. The book is not intended to be a review of all educational research literature on a single concept. Our applications filtered out the very best new ideas from the most relevant research articles coming from a large number of sources.

While experience is a great teacher, there are faster, more humane, and more efficient means of teaching and learning, which coupled with experience become empowering, effective, rewarding, and beneficial. The purpose of this book is to give a voice to the research and the researchers who create the questions about how special learners learn most effectively. Filtered through our own experiences in schools, we hope to make the valuable products of their inquiry available to all those involved in teaching students who need additional supports to facilitate their learning.

This book is not meant to be read as one would read a novel, but rather our objective is to focus on useful and practical educational research that translates into a range of choices and solutions to individual teaching and learning problems typically faced by teachers working with diverse learners. Within these chapters we present a large range of instructional strategies and suggestions based on educational, psychological, and sociological studies. The strategies are based on research conducted with teachers and students. Strategies within the chapters are structured in a user-friendly format:

- Strategy: A simple, concise, or crisp statement of an instructional strategy.
- What the Research Says: A brief discussion of the research that led to the strategy. This section should simply give the teacher some confidence in, and a deeper understanding of, the principle(s) being discussed as an instructional strategy.
- Application: A description of how this teaching strategy can be used in instructional settings.
- Precautions and Possible Pitfalls: Caveats intended to make possible reasonably flawless implementation of the teaching strategy. We try to help teachers avoid common difficulties before they occur.
- Sources: These are provided so that the reader may refer to the original research to discover in more detail the main points of the strategies, research, and classroom applications.

It is our hope that if those new to teaching students with disabilities accept some of these ideas, maybe they can avoid the "sink or swim" mentality that many of us experienced when we first started. We can make the "learning curve" less steep in those first few years. Veterans can also benefit from knowledge gained from the most recent research. Given the critical need for teachers now and in the future, we, as a profession, cannot afford to have potentially good teachers leaving the profession because they don't feel supported, feel too overwhelmed, or suffer from early burnout or disillusionment.

For teachers reading this book for the first time, there may be strategies that apparently don't apply. As in many new endeavors, there may be a tendency to "not know what you don't know." We ask that you come back and revisit this book from time to time throughout the year. What may not be applicable the first time you read it may be of help at a later date. Veterans can refresh their teaching toolbox by scanning the range of strategies presented in the book and applying these strategies to their own classroom environment.

Teaching, and education in general, have never been more exciting or more challenging. Expectations for teachers, students, and schools continue to rise. The more resources teachers have at their fingertips to assist their practice along their educational journey, the better the outcome for us all. We hope all teachers will find this book useful and practical in defining and enhancing their teaching skills.

Sarah J. McNary
Neal A. Glasgow
Cathy D. Hicks

Acknowledgments

We are grateful to the people at Corwin Press, especially Faye Zucker, Stacy Wagner, and Cyndee Callan for their complete collaboration and support.

Sarah McNary is indebted to coauthors Cathy Hicks and Neal Glasgow for their ongoing confidence and unwavering support. Their dedication to educational practice based on research rather than fashion is an inspiration. Deepest appreciation is due to the students with and without disabilities that she has worked with over the years. Working with all of them has been an honor and a delight. She has learned more about teaching from them than from anything covered in her training coursework. Loving gratitude goes to her husband, Dave, and her children, Erica and Alex, for their confidence. Last, her deepest thanks go to her mum for her gentle support; and her sisters, Jacqueline and Caroline, who are always ready and willing to listen as well as offer their help and solutions.

Neal Glasgow gratefully acknowledges the many special education teachers he has worked with over his career. As a career mainstream teacher, which includes a short journey into "ESL" science, one of his roles in special education has been that of an educational consumer. Everything he has learned about learning disabilities, accommodations, and everything in between has come from very knowledgeable and dedicated special education teachers. Their dedication and professionalism stand out among their educational peers. Further, and most important, he acknowledges and thanks his coauthors, Sarah McNary and Cathy Hicks, for their insightful and professional contributions to this book, personal touch on the world of special education, and their good humor. Because of them the messages in the book truly come from the trenches of real teaching. Their writing gives the academic research a real-world validity and usefulness. Finally, he acknowledges Tommy O., his first mainstreamed student with a learning disability. Tommy fostered a rewarding beginning to the world of individual learning styles and the accommodation of differences.

Cathy Hicks is grateful and in awe of the exceptional special education teachers she has been privileged to work with over the past 30 years. These teachers are "angels on earth." The skill, passion, enthusiasm, patience, and love they possess are nothing short of incredible. A giant among these special teachers is Sarah McNary, someone she is proud to call friend and colleague. Sarah knows absolutely everything about special education. More important, she has never met a student she didn't like. Sarah is an invaluable resource to teachers of students with special needs. Cathy also acknowledges the expertise and dedication of coauthor Neal Glasgow. The writing team spent many hours engaged in meaningful and interesting dialogue, all the while proving that there is no "magic bullet" for teaching students with disabilities. A final thank you to Cathy's daughter Summer, for teaching her the unique challenges a child with special needs brings to a family. Having been Summer's mother has made her a better, more patient, and compassionate teacher. The experience brought home the truth that every child has special gifts and talents to share.

Corwin Press and the authors extend their thanks to the following reviewers for their contributions to this volume:

Millie Gore, Ed.D.
Midwestern State University
Wichita Falls, TX

Toby Karten
Manalapan Englishtown Regional Schools
Manalapan, NJ

J. David Smith
University of Virginia's College at Wise
Wise, VA

Jacqueline Thousand
Cal State San Marcos
San Marcos, CA

About the Authors

Sarah J. McNary is currently teaching a credit recovery program for the San Dieguito Union High School District in Southern California, where she is also the district's consultant for special education working with the Beginning Teacher Support and Assessment (BTSA)/Induction program. She is a faculty member in the Master of Education program for the University of Phoenix. Over the last 15 years she has taught SH, SDC, RSP, and general education classes at the elementary, middle school, and high school levels. She is a frequent presenter on a variety of aspects of special education and student support, and coauthor with Cathy Hicks and Neal Glasgow of *What Successful Mentors Do: 81 Research-Based Strategies for New Teacher Induction, Training, and Support* (Corwin Press, 2004). She is innately curious and is a firm believer in life-long learning. When asked what she teaches, Sarah will answer, "Kids"; when asked what she teaches kids, she responds, "Life! I just use my curriculum to do it!" She and her husband split their time between Encinitas and their mountain home. She is also the mother of two teenagers.

Neal A. Glasgow has been involved in education on many levels. His experience includes serving as a secondary school science and art teacher both in California and New York, as a university biotechnology teaching laboratory director and laboratory technician, as an educational consultant, and as a frequent educational speaker on many topics. He is the author or coauthor of six books on educational topics: *What Successful Mentors Do: 81 Research-Based Strategies for New Teacher Induction, Training, and Support* (2004); *What Successful Teachers Do: 91 Research-Based Strategies for New and Veteran Teachers* (2003); *Tips for the Science Teacher: Research-Based Strategies to Help Students Learn* (2001); *New Curriculum for New Times: A Guide to Student-Centered Problem-Based Learning* (1997); *Doing*

Science: Innovative Curriculum Beyond the Textbook for the Life Science Classroom (1997); and *Taking the Classroom Into the Community: A Guide Book* (1996). Neal is currently teaching AP art history and art at San Dieguito Academy High School, a California public high school of choice, and continues to do research and write on educational topics as well as work on various art projects. He is married, the father of two grown sons, and the grandfather of one grandson.

Cathy D. Hicks is currently the Beginning Teacher Support and Assessment (BTSA)/Induction Coordinator for the San Dieguito Union High School District in Southern California. She oversees a two-year induction program for new teachers. She is the coauthor of *What Successful Mentors Do: 81 Research-Based Strategies for New Teacher Induction, Training, and Support* (2004) and *What Successful Teachers Do: 91 Research-Based Classroom Strategies for New and Veteran Teachers* (2003). Cathy serves on the Executive Board of the California Association of School Health Educators (CASHE) and is on the adjunct faculty of California State University, San Marcos, teaching methods courses for teachers completing their credentials. She has presented at more than a dozen mentor-teacher leader conferences. Cathy has taught at both the middle and high school levels for over 27 years. During that time she was involved in the California State Mentor Teacher Program and has been mentoring new teachers in her district for more than 19 years. Her energy, enthusiasm, and passion for teaching and supporting new teachers reinforce the career path she chose in elementary school. She believes the most effective teachers are the ones who never settle for "good enough" but continue to grow, stretch, reflect, create, collaborate, and take risks throughout their teaching careers. Cathy is married and has two grown children and one adorable granddaughter.

1

Interacting With Students

The secret of education lies in respecting the pupil.

—Emerson

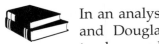 **STRATEGY 1: Use a "hypothesis and frequent reflection" strategy when working with students who have special education needs.**

What the Research Says

 In an analysis of 19 expert special educators, Stough, Palmer, and Douglas (2003) determined that the success of these teachers and their students with special needs could be attributed to their unique approach and application of pedagogical knowledge. The central finding of this study was that each teacher was concerned about individual student performance.

These teachers had a minimum of five years' experience and were evaluated using a multifaceted approach (interviewing, videotaping, observation, stimulated recall, and field notes). The study was conducted in five schools ranging from urban to rural and elementary through high school levels. In addition, the special education needs of the students varied along the continuum of services (RSP, MM, ED, etc.).

Considering first the academic behavior and then the classroom behavior, each teacher used a hypothesis/reflection strategy to teach his or her students. By using prior knowledge of the individual student, each teacher developed a hypothesis about the student and then an instructional plan to meet those individual needs. During the instruction, the teacher would assess the individual student's progress and reflect on the efficacy of the practice in that moment, making any needed adjustments. The teachers believed strongly that all students could learn and were collectively working to increase student independence and emotional well-being.

Application

 Expert teachers know that it is essential to consider the individual student. Novice teachers may be able to cite this concept but will benefit from a supported hypothesis/reflection approach. By using stimulated recall and collegial reflection, all teachers can adjust their practice to increase student learning.

Individual teachers would benefit from taking the time to review available data (IEP, 504, cumulative file, etc.) to develop a basic profile of a student and his or her individual strengths and weaknesses. Using background pedagogical knowledge of instructional practice, the teacher can then form a hypothesis about how that student will benefit most from specific instruction. As the instruction unfolds, the teacher will note the student's response and can adjust the practice as needed.

Often, by considering the needs of one student, a teacher can positively impact an entire class. For example, if a teacher notices that an individual student needs to have written directions read aloud due to a processing delay, the teacher may discover that the entire class performs better when she reviews the instructions orally with the whole class prior to beginning an assignment.

Frequent reflection is the key to evaluating the hypothesis and determining the efficacy of instructional practice. With time and experience, teachers' knowledge of student characteristics increases along with the number of instructional strategies they are able to employ.

Precautions and Possible Pitfalls

It is important that teachers base their hypotheses about individual students on facts or observable behaviors. It can be tempting to assume that because a student has the same disability as another student their instructional needs are the same. The key to excellence in teaching students with special needs is to consider the student individually. It can also be tempting to do what has always been done rather than design a practice that specifically meets an individual's need. By constructively using assessment and subsequent reflection to inform their practice, teachers can accelerate their students' success.

Source

Stough, L. M., Palmer, D., & Douglas, J. (2003). Special thinking in special settings: A qualitative study of expert special educators. *Journal of Special Education, 36*(4), 206–223.

 STRATEGY 2: Pre-teach general education students with instructional strategies prior to forming cooperative groups.

What the Research Says

 Two studies were conducted to assess the efficacy of cooperative learning groups for students with autism (Kamps et al., 2002). The studies included a control group with no specific peer interaction, a cooperative group with specific learning objectives, and a social skills group with less formal guidelines. Student attention was measured over the course of a year and the results showed a significant increase in attention and social skills acquisition in both the social skills group and the cooperative group. The target students increased their attention from below 30 seconds to over 191 seconds measured in 5-minute probes. In addition, the students in the social skills group and the cooperative group increased their interactions with others more than three times the baseline. The researchers determined that the efficacy increased when the peers were trained in effective instructional strategies. Understanding teaching techniques like modeling, reinforcement, visual cuing, scripts, and natural settings significantly contributed to student success.

Application

 Although most teachers are aware that pre-teaching procedures prior to introducing a new activity to their students increases success, few teachers take the next step. By specifically teaching basic techniques like modeling and reinforcement, all students can benefit from a supported cooperative group experience. For the student with a disability, the need for a positive group is even stronger and often harder to come by.

Teachers should identify the specific instructional needs of their students with disabilities and what instructional approaches appear to be the most effective. They should then teach those skills to the whole class. For example, consider the student with a processing delay who benefits from visual cuing. A teacher could teach the entire class about the benefits of using visual aids when giving presentations or working to persuade an audience. Examples of visual cuing in the media could be discussed, and students could create their own examples. In-class examples of visual cuing could be highlighted, like homework listed on a daily agenda, check-off sheets for projects, clean-up activities, and so on. When students participate in cooperative groups, they can now incorporate these skills to facilitate their own communication and particularly the involvement of the student with a disability.

Precautions and Possible Pitfalls

 It is important that teachers do not rely so heavily on a few capable students to constantly facilitate the efforts of a student with a disability. Likewise, when planning for the student with a disability, it is common to stick with what has worked in the past. Teachers need to branch out and try a variety of approaches to help expand their students' capabilities.

Source

Kamps, D., Potucek, J., Dugan, E., Kravitz, T., Gonzalez-Lopez, A., Garcia, J., et al. (2002). Peer training to facilitate social interaction for elementary students with autism and their peers. *Exceptional Children, 68*(2), 173–188.

 STRATEGY 3: Use creativity to design ways to academically support and challenge students with severe disabilities who are included in general education classrooms.

What the Research Says

 Although many students with learning disabilities are successfully included in general education classes for both academic and social growth, frequently IEP teams limit their expectations of students with severe disabilities. Most students with severe disabilities are placed primarily for social goals, and any academic expectation is limited to the life-skill training that occurs in the special education classroom (Downing & Echinger, 2003). Creative teachers can identify myriad ways to assist students with severe disabilities to work on their academic goals. Use of pictorial charts and number cards can provide a bridge for students. Downing and Echinger offer the example of a student in a biology class who sorts and counts seeds while nondisabled peers identify the genus. When the class is working on writing a story, the student with a severe disability might select pictures that would illustrate the story. Students learning how to follow directions and interact socially might be called on to distribute papers or collect homework routinely. They offer additional suggestions for teachers who use random groupings of students for specific activities. Students with severe disabilities could use pictures of the class and a die to place students' names into envelopes, forming groups (with the assistance of a paraeducator) while the teacher is delivering the lecture.

Application

 The first step in creating appropriate academic activities for a student with severe disabilities is to consider the student's IEP goals. With those goals in mind, the next step is to open a dialogue regarding the specific curriculum as well as the classroom procedures of the specific class. Some teachers find it helpful to create a chart that blocks out the basics of these two areas so they can be viewed simultaneously to begin the planning process. Either by viewing the chart, or simply by reviewing the IEP and lesson plan book, teachers should consider the crossover points that could be avenues for appropriate learning activities for the student. They should begin with the classroom procedures and evaluate things like homework turn-in, group activities, lectures versus labs, and so on. Teachers should look for opportunities for the student to practice his or her academic goals (writing name, recognizing routines, etc.), then move to the curriculum itself. Teachers must consider the essential standards that are being addressed by the specific unit and the level of modification that is appropriate for the specific student. If the student has the services of a paraeducator during the general education class, teachers should ensure that he or she is aware of both the curricular and individual student's goals for the lesson.

Precautions and Possible Pitfalls

Teachers should avoid contrived matches of curriculum and academic goals. The more real and relevant the activity is, the more likely it is to benefit the student's growth overall. Making a collage of food groups might be appropriate for a nutrition or biology class but not for history. It is essential that the standards for the lesson are addressed and that alternate activities don't become "busywork." Teachers should also be aware of any safety or medical issues that could negatively influence specific activities.

Source

Downing, J. E., & Eichinger, J. (2003). Creating learning opportunities for students with severe disabilities in inclusive classrooms. *Teaching Exceptional Children, 36*(1), 26–32.

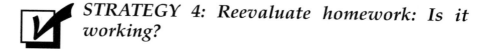

STRATEGY 4: Reevaluate homework: Is it working?

What the Research Says

In their book, Etta Kralovec and John Buell present a unique view of the homework concept and question the value of the practice itself (Buell & Kralovec, 2000). Few studies have been conducted on the subject, and while the book offers perspectives from both sides of the debate, it is clear that the homework concept needs to be examined more closely. For example, Buell and Kralovec cite homework as a great discriminator as children, once leaving school for the day, encounter a range of parental supports, challenging home environments, afterschool jobs and sports, and a mix of resources available to some and not to others. Clearly, opportunities are not equal. Tired parents are held captive by the demands of their children's school, unable to develop their own priorities for family life. And for a student with a disability, parents may lack the needed skills to help with homework.

The questions their research and discourse explores are, "With single parent households becoming more common or with both parents working, is it reasonable to accept the homework concept, as it is now practiced, as useful and valid considering the tradeoffs families need to make?" "How does homework contribute to family dynamics in negative or positive ways?" "Does it unnecessarily stifle other important opportunities or create an uneven or unequal playing field for some students?"

Buell and Kralovec also provide examples of communities that have tried to formalize homework policy as the communities tried to balance the demands of homework with extracurricular activities and the need for family time. They also point out the aspects of inequity inherent in the fact that many students lack the resources at home to compete on an equal footing with those peers who have computers, Internet access, highly educated parents, unlimited funds, and other resources for homework requirements.

They also point out that homework persists despite the lack of any solid evidence that it achieves its much-touted gains. Homework is one of our most entrenched institutional practices, yet one of the least investigated. It is also the one least likely to be completed by students with disabilities unless assisted by parents, tutors, or friends.

Application

Teachers should be aware of the inequalities that may exist among students in their classes regarding their ability to complete homework assignments. Certain students may be excluded from the opportunities for support and other resources. Consider the following questions:

What is homework?

How much homework is too much?

What are or should be the purposes of homework?

Can different assignments be given to different students in the same class?

Do students have specific accommodations or modifications regarding homework written in their IEP or 504 plans?

Do all students have equal opportunities to successfully complete the homework?

Who is responsible for homework, the students or the parents?

Do all students have the same capacity to self-regulate?

How are other school activities or family-based responsibilities factored in?

What is the best and most equitable way to deal with overachievers?

Is the homework load balanced between teachers?

When designing homework assignments, particularly those that are multistep or project based, consider consulting a special educator for suggestions on making the assignment manageable for students with disabilities. Frequently teachers have no concept of "too much" or "too little" when it comes to homework.

Precautions and Possible Pitfalls

Traditionally, homework has been seen as a solution to rather than the cause of educational problems. It takes a little bit of acclimation time to begin to look at the homework concept with a new lens. However, the value of homework in providing opportunities for students to deepen their knowledge should not be ignored. Be wary of assuming a specific assignment is "easy" for students. For example, picking up a book from the library and bringing it to class may be a 5-minute operation for most students. However, for a student with disabilities who may be unfamiliar with the organization of a library (including accessing the computerized catalog, locating the appropriate selections in the stacks, and then skimming several books to select the best one), this may be beyond the scope of his or her ability without specific assistance. Consider setting a fixed time limit for certain homework projects, as appropriate.

Source

Buell, J., & Kralovec, E. (2000). *The end of homework: How homework disrupts families, overburdens children, and limits learning.* Boston: Beacon.

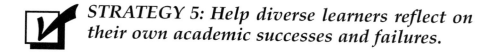

STRATEGY 5: *Help diverse learners reflect on their own academic successes and failures.*

What the Research Says

Students often get into ruts in school, falsely thinking that because they didn't do well in a class in the past, they won't now or in the future. However, extensive research shows that students can learn to control their own academic destinies. One body of research focuses on students' attributions for success and failure (Alderman, 1990). This research shows there are four common reasons people give for their successes and failures: ability, effort, task difficulty, and luck. Attributions can be divided into two dimensions: stable-unstable and internal-external. Stable-unstable refers to how consistent the attributions are over time. That is, the extent to which a person uses the same types of reasons to explain his or her success or failure over and over again (stable) or whether the person gives one kind of reason on one occasion and another type of reason another time (unstable). For example, a student says solving mass problems in physics is always too difficult for her (stable) but that in chemistry some balancing equation problems are easy for her and some are too difficult (unstable). Stable arguments are often harder to address. They tend to be avoidance arguments; that is, the student consistently uses the same argument to avoid work he or she feels threatened by. Older students tend to form defensive "stable" arguments to avoid potential "failure" situations.

Internal-external refers to a situation in which a person assigns responsibility for his or her successes and failures—inside or outside the self. For example, a student says she didn't do well on her test about the Holocaust because she didn't study enough (internal). She says she didn't do well on her first science test because her family interfered with her study time (external). She says she got a good grade on her second science test because she was lucky (external).

Students' explanations of their successes and failures have important consequences for future performance on academic tasks. Research shows there are four common ways students explain their successes and failures: effort ("I could do it if I really tried"), ability ("I'm just not a good writer"), luck ("I guessed right"), and task difficulty ("The test was too hard") (Alderman, 1990). Attributions are related to the following:

- Expectations about one's likelihood of success
- Judgments about one's ability
- Emotional reactions of pride, hopelessness, and helplessness
- Willingness to work hard and self-regulate one's efforts

Application

Help diverse learners rid themselves of their misconceptions about learning. Students who see a relationship between their effort and their success are more likely to use learning strategies such as organizing, planning, goal setting, self-checking, and self-instruction. Alderman's "links to success" model is designed to help at-risk students develop attributions that will motivate them to succeed. Her four links to success are as follows:

1. Proximal goals, which are short term rather than long term, specific rather than general, and hard (but reachable) rather than easy; for example, "This week I'll manage my time so that I have three extra hours to study." For the student with disabilities, the time frame for proximal goals may need to be shortened. Depending on the student's individual needs, consider goals measured in 15-minute, half hour, period, or daily increments. Teach students to anticipate and overcome obstacles, monitor progress while goals are being pursued, and evaluate whether they achieved their goals at the end of the specified time. "I'll know whether I accomplished this goal by writing down how much time I study and

comparing that to how much I studied last week." A possible obstacle to achieving this goal is making a statement such as, "I will overcome these obstacles by . . ." If they don't achieve their goals, teach students to determine why and what they could do differently next time.

2. Learning strategies, which students are taught so they can apply effective strategies such as summarizing and clarifying, emphasize meaningful learning and can be used across subjects and situations. Ineffective approaches, such as repetition, which tends to emphasize rote memorization, can be difficult for students with learning disabilities—particularly those with short-term memory issues.

3. Success experiences have students evaluate their success in achieving their proximal goals and focus on learning ("How much progress did I make?") rather than performance ("What grade did I get?") as the goal.

4. Attributions for success encourage students to explain their successes in terms of their personal efforts or abilities. The teacher's role here is to give students feedback on why they succeeded or failed and help students give the appropriate explanation. Was an answer incorrect, incomplete, or was there a careless mistake? Make sure students understand why an answer is incorrect. Ask questions such as, "What did you do when you tried to answer that question or solve that problem?"

Precautions and Possible Pitfalls

Feelings of helplessness are created over a period of time through the belief that failure is due to lack of ability, so it is important for students to learn that their ability can improve if they use proper strategies and make appropriate efforts. This is particularly important when dealing with students who have a heightened sensitivity to their own learning issues. Students want to resist being put in positions of failure and are often more motivated by fear of failure than by the "new" strategies for success. Occasionally, and usually with older students, some efforts simply won't work. Don't give up on all students because a few have given up on themselves. Be careful not to alienate those few because they aren't buying in.

Source

Alderman, M. K. (1990, September). Motivation for at-risk students. *Educational Leadership*, 27–30.

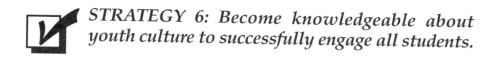

STRATEGY 6: Become knowledgeable about youth culture to successfully engage all students.

What the Research Says

 It is no secret that some of the most difficult challenges facing teachers are classroom management, physical and emotional isolation, and difficulty adapting to the needs and abilities of their students.

Brock and Grady (1997) concluded, "Teaching is one of the few careers in which the least experienced members face the greatest challenges and responsibilities" (p. 11). Many teachers come prepared with book knowledge and theory, but the reality of controlling a classroom of 35 students is a whole other story. This reality usually hits after the first few weeks of school, when the honeymoon period is over for the students and they have figured out what they can and can't get away with in a particular class. This is particularly true for students with disabilities.

In many teacher preparation, induction, and mentoring programs across the nation, these issues are being addressed with concrete solutions and qualified mentors. Connecting with exemplary veteran teachers who have experience and rapport with adolescents can also be a big help. Teachers at the secondary level reported their teacher colleagues having a positive influence in helping them understand the challenges of adolescents. Elementary teachers felt their principals were extremely helpful in providing support and encouragement.

Application

No longer can we tolerate a "sink or swim" attitude. In California, the BTSA (Beginning Teacher Support and Assessment) program focuses in on beginning teachers learning as much as possible about the students in their classrooms. Knowing which languages are spoken at home, previous student test scores, the community in which these students live, and cultural and socioeconomic backgrounds all help teachers understand and adapt to the needs of the students they teach. Excellent classroom managers do this instinctively as they prepare their curriculum for their students, often on a class-by-class basis.

Understanding where students are and what is important to them is a vital first step in designing instruction. Check literature, music, clothing trends, and so on. Spend time looking over popular magazines, check on students' favorite films and television shows, and most importantly, take time to talk to and listen to them. Some teachers distribute interest inventories at the start of the school year to help learn about their students. These can also be used as a reflection tool at the end of the year for students as they note how much they have changed. Relating the curriculum to the students in order to make it meaningful, relevant, and fun reduces classroom management issues as well as contributes to student success.

Precautions and Possible Pitfalls

 With the social climate today and students coming to class with myriad challenges and concerns, it is more important than ever for teachers to be aware of the problems and challenges of adolescent culture. What may seem trivial to an adult can be monumental to an adolescent. Many students would rather be considered "bad" than "stupid" in front of their peers. Yet many times a teacher will put a student in the position of acting out because the student doesn't know the answer to a question. Be careful not to judge students based on what other teachers say. All students deserve a teacher who has not made up his or her mind about what the student is capable of in the classroom. Be careful of becoming too much of a "buddy" or "friend"— retain adult status and model adult ideas and behavior. The more a teacher can invest in understanding his or her students, where they are coming from, and what is important to them, the more successful the teacher can be in implementing classroom management procedures.

Sources

Brock, B. L., & Grady, M. L. (1997). *From first-year to first-rate: Principals guiding beginning teachers.* Thousand Oaks, CA: Corwin.

Lortie, D. C. (1975). *Schoolteacher: A sociological study.* Chicago: University of Chicago.

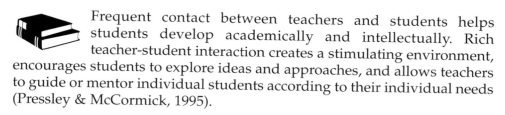

STRATEGY 7: Remember that students with special needs benefit most from one-on-one contact.

What the Research Says

 Frequent contact between teachers and students helps students develop academically and intellectually. Rich teacher-student interaction creates a stimulating environment, encourages students to explore ideas and approaches, and allows teachers to guide or mentor individual students according to their individual needs (Pressley & McCormick, 1995).

Application

Working with individual students in a traditional classroom setting for long periods of time is not practical. While students are working individually on an exercise, the teacher should visit with individual students and offer them some meaningful suggestions. Such suggestions might include hints for moving a student who appears frustrated or bogged down on a point toward a solution.

These private comments to students might also be in the form of advice regarding the format of the student's work. That is, some students are their own worst enemy when they are doing a geometry problem and working with a diagram which is either so small that they cannot do anything worthwhile with it or so inaccurately drawn that it, too, proves to be relatively useless. Such small support offerings will move students along and give them that very important feeling of teacher interest.

In some cases, when a student experiences more severe problems, the teacher might be wise to work with the student after class time during the school day. In this situation, it would be advisable to have the student describe the work as it is being done, trying to justify his or her procedure and explain concepts. During such one-on-one tutoring sessions, the teacher can get a good insight into the student's problems. Are they conceptual? Has the student missed understanding an algorithm? Does the student have perceptual difficulties or spatial difficulties? And so on.

Precautions and Possible Pitfalls

Working with individual students and merely making perfunctory comments when more might be expected could be useless if the severity of the problem might warrant more attention. Teachers should make every effort to give proper attention to students when attempting to implement this teaching strategy. Teachers should keep the student's level in mind so that, where appropriate, they can add some spice to the individual sessions by providing a carefully selected range and choice of challenges to the student in order to further individualize the learning process. Make sure advanced students don't get bored. Challenge them by giving them more difficult problems to solve, having them tutor other students, or having them evaluate alternative approaches to solving a problem.

Be aware that some students can become very needy. They often lack confidence or the ability to work comfortably in an independent manner. This can compel them to begin to dominate the teacher's time. When this occurs, teachers should give them the same general attention they give to others. When their demands begin to dominate the class, invite them to meet after school or at a time when they can have undivided attention. To conserve time, consider combining a few students with similar problems and address their needs together. Or, have students who understand the material serve as tutors, mentors, or group leaders.

Source

Pressley, M., & McCormick, C. (1995). *Advanced Educational Psychology.* New York: HarperCollins.

 STRATEGY 8: Explore any hidden stereotypes and perceptions about included students with learning disabilities.

What the Research Says

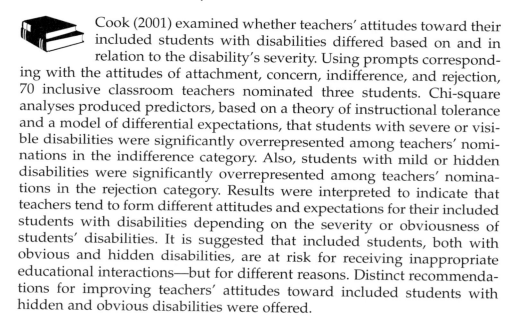Cook (2001) examined whether teachers' attitudes toward their included students with disabilities differed based on and in relation to the disability's severity. Using prompts corresponding with the attitudes of attachment, concern, indifference, and rejection, 70 inclusive classroom teachers nominated three students. Chi-square analyses produced predictors, based on a theory of instructional tolerance and a model of differential expectations, that students with severe or visible disabilities were significantly overrepresented among teachers' nominations in the indifference category. Also, students with mild or hidden disabilities were significantly overrepresented among teachers' nominations in the rejection category. Results were interpreted to indicate that teachers tend to form different attitudes and expectations for their included students with disabilities depending on the severity or obviousness of students' disabilities. It is suggested that included students, both with obvious and hidden disabilities, are at risk for receiving inappropriate educational interactions—but for different reasons. Distinct recommendations for improving teachers' attitudes toward included students with hidden and obvious disabilities were offered.

Application

Teacher-student communication should be primarily focused on instructional interaction. Often, with some groups and individuals, the instructional interactions focus on behavioral or disciplinary interactions and away from the more appropriate and purposeful types of educational interactions. Teachers become attached to some students and student groups and place others in categories of concern, indifference, or total rejection (as described in the research). All teachers make judgments, interpret situations, and form attitudes regarding instructional tolerance of groups and individuals.

The bottom line is that inappropriate perceptions of disabilities influence the attitudes teachers hold toward their included students with learning disabilities. This results in changes in the frequency, duration, expectation, and quality of teacher-student interactions.

Bias and stereotyping can be very subtle and come from a place very deep in the subconscious. Once teachers think about it or are made aware of it they can develop personal action plans to change these patterns of behavior and implement more objective ways of creating meaningful and effective educational interactions.

Self-education is the key. Sharing ideas with trusted colleagues or talking it over with a favorite special education teacher allows teachers to see themselves and their included students in a more objective light. Once they are made aware of their possible bias or stereotyping, they are glad to replace those ideas with more useful and accurate lenses with which to view students. Bias and stereotyping are usually very personal, and only new knowledge frees them from these notions. Developing more accurate and useful ways of seeing students is a powerful strategy to increase teachers' abilities to meet the needs of all students.

Precautions and Possible Pitfalls

No real pitfalls here. Becoming more aware of the personal factors and mindsets that influence teachers' decision making about students is always a positive thing.

Source

Cook, B. G. (2001). A comparison of teachers' attitude toward their students with mild and severe disabilities. *Journal of Special Education, 34*(4), 203.

 STRATEGY 9: Learn how to facilitate the social acceptance of students with special needs in general education classes.

What the Research Says

The inclusion of students with moderate and severe disabilities in a general education classroom was established under the humanitarian premise that their interactions would lead to greater acceptance and understanding of students with special needs in society in general. Also, students with special needs would benefit from a wider range of social and academic opportunities. Unfortunately, in some settings the idealistic assumption behind inclusion is often undermined. Students with moderate and severe disabilities are often socially ostracized, especially in adolescence. Social acceptance is fundamental to the quality of life of all people, including those with disabilities; this study sought to determine what barriers exist to inclusion of adolescents with disabilities in their school peer groups.

Sparling (2002) conducted a qualitative study consisting of a survey of 534 senior high students (grades 9–12). It was undertaken to determine factors that affect the social acceptance of students with moderate and severe disabilities at senior high school. The nature of the student's disability, social and cultural influences, teacher attitude and modeling, as well as adolescent psychology and peer pressure are all cited as issues that affect inclusion. Researchers found that the social inclusion of students is hampered by several factors including:

1. Lack of knowledge about disabilities, which leads to fear and uncertainty about how to interact with students

2. Peer pressure, which discourages students from interacting with their classmates with disabilities

3. School and community culture, which values success and achievement

4. Nature of the student's disability, which hampers traditional communication and may also lead to inappropriate social interactions

5. Teacher attitude, which determines the tone of the class, and therefore the degree of acceptance of students

While researchers found that students with special needs are accepted in certain situations at senior high school, they found there is room for improvement through education and encouragement of nondisabled students and staff at the school.

In this study, 82% of the general education students indicated they would help a student with special needs if asked by a teacher or teacher assistant. Ten percent stated they would not. Also, 60% said they would interact more if the teacher or teaching assistant explained how better to relate to students with special needs. Sixty-eight percent of the students in this study felt that students with physical or intellectual disabilities would fit in better socially if students knew more about the disabilities. Again, knowledge appears to be the primary factor affecting social inclusion of students with disabilities (Sparling, 2002).

Application

Out of the five main points highlighted in the conclusion in the research, teachers have the most control over the lack of knowledge about disabilities, leading to fear and uncertainty, and teacher attitude, which determines the tone of the class and therefore the degree of acceptance of students.

Knowledge is the key to inclusion of students with disabilities. It decreases fear and diminishes the stereotypes associated with people with moderate and severe disabilities, thereby facilitating their social inclusion. Teachers as well as students can benefit from increased knowledge. In most secondary school settings, students with special needs are assigned to classes and there is very little support or education that comes along with the students. Teachers may get an IEP that helps, but for the most part they are on their own in trying to prepare for the wide range of support students require. There are a few special education teachers out there who understand that position, and they will take the time to include real suggestions for accommodations based on their firsthand knowledge and experience with the students. This is an exceptional teacher but not the norm. If this isn't common practice at their site, teachers should take their list of students and visit each case manager and ask for relevant information early in the semester or school year.

Sparling's (2002) study indicates that many teachers have a positive attitude toward inclusion but most expressed concerns regarding the lack of training to effectively teach students with disabilities and classes that included them. The study also identified the greatest threat students with disabilities bring to classrooms—the threat to classroom norms. Most teachers believe they are fair and nice to special education students but need to optimize their knowledge to better build action plans and anticipate problems and potential solutions before issues come up.

Also, add "getting to know the parents" to the list of factors to discuss with case managers. Often case managers can also give tips on how to optimize home-school interactions. Informed teachers and student peers are more accepting of students with disabilities with added knowledge. They are also more accepting of any anomalies exhibited by these students.

Teacher attitude affects and influences how general education students see students with disabilities. How do students see teacher interactions with these students? If they knew more about how to interact with students with disabilities would they be more accepting? Is the teacher a good role model? How can the teacher assist his or her students to play a role in fostering inclusion? A lack of knowledge about how to communicate, and about the nature of student disabilities, leads to fear and decreased acceptance, which affects social inclusion. It's clear that increasing the knowledge of all students can have a positive effect on acceptance.

Knowledge transfer can take many forms, but for an individual teacher in the confines of his or her own classroom, carefully modeling positive behaviors and informally educating general education students seem to be good strategies. By engaging in subtle conversations with selected students, peer leaders, and those most receptive, teachers can start to "break the ice" for those reluctant but receptive students. Most of this can be handled informally as needs arise.

If knowledge is the key to inclusion, then teachers are in the best position to use their creativity to develop effective strategies to make it work!

Precautions and Possible Pitfalls

Time is always a factor. What are teachers going to take out of their daily teaching load in order to add additional strategies that foster inclusion? Research indicates inclusion is a fast-growing educational strategy and evidence continues to mount in support of the positive effects of inclusive education for all students. If this is the case, developing sensitivity and strategies that foster successful and effective inclusion are essential. As teachers become better at inclusion they become better overall teachers.

Sources

Katz, J., & Mirenda, P. (2002). Including students with developmental disabilities in general education classrooms: Social benefits. *International Journal of Special Education, 17*(2), 14–24.

Sparling, E. (2002). Social acceptance at senior high school. *International Journal of Special Education, 17*(1), 91–100.

 STRATEGY 10: Develop specific pedagogies, behavioral management techniques, and interventions to assist in working with students with attention deficit/hyperactivity disorder (ADHD).

What the Research Says

McLaughlin and Reiber (2004) describe some of the more commonly used in-school treatments and evaluate their effectiveness for ADHD. These researchers found in their recent comprehensive review that there are currently three treatments for ADHD that can be considered supported by research: (1) psychostimulant medications, (2) behavioral intervention, and (3) a combination of these two. A significant amount of research has been conducted that supports the combination of these two interventions in the treatment of ADHD.

The researchers' work went on to explore a variety of classroom interventions to assist teachers in working successfully with children with ADHD. They included: classroom structure, teaching modifications, peer interventions, token economies, and self-management. The interventions reviewed and described were scaled from the basic modifications needed in the classroom to those in which more time and resources were involved. All the strategies reviewed were based on qualitative research.

Investigators found and stated that discussion of alternative treatments is practical for three reasons.

1. ADHD does not have its own disability designation for special education intervention. This means that with the exception of an Other Health Impaired designation, ADHD is predominately addressed in the general education classroom (Heward, 2003).

2. While recommendations of medication treatment for an ADHD student may be discussed in a meeting involving instructors, the decision surrounding this approach is not one for the instructor to make and should be left to the student's physician and parents.

3. Classroom interventions and attempts at behavioral intervention are solely in the hands and guidance of the classroom instructor. From a general education perspective, many times this falls on the general education instructor to ensure a healthy learning environment for the entire class. At times, the least prepared professionals are working with ADHD students.

Application

Attention deficit/hyperactivity disorder is characterized by significant problems with attention, impulsiveness, and overactivity. According to the background information in McLaughlin and Reiber's (2004) article, it is one of the most common reasons for referral of children to mental health clinics and affects an estimated 3% to 5% of the elementary school-age population. On average, these estimates place at least one child with ADHD in every classroom in America. For this reason, the use of effective interventions for reducing the classroom impairment characteristics of students with ADHD is important to all school personnel. Three intervention strategies were suggested by the research.

1. Classroom Structure

The general characteristics of ADHD are inattention, high distractibility and impulsivity, and hyperactivity. These traits make concentrating on schoolwork, instruction, and learning very difficult. To be successful academically, students with ADHD must be able to focus their attention on the instructor and the lesson. Therefore, students with ADHD benefit greatly from an orderly environment carefully constructed with them in mind. For this reason, classroom structure is one of the most important areas of instructor influence in the classroom. The use of classroom structure to alleviate the effects of ADHD in the classroom has received much attention and research support. Classroom structure can be divided into two distinct categories, physical structure and mental organizational structure. Some suggestions and information to consider are:

- Closed classrooms with walls and windows are more conducive than open classrooms where students can see other teachers with other groups of students.
- Trends toward learning communities and groups of students at tables produce more distractions than desks.
- Traditional desks in straight rows work best.
- Reduce clutter in the room. Disorganized rooms, unfinished projects, and wall-to-wall displays are a problem.
- Place students with ADHD in the front or middle of desk rows away from external distractions such as pencil sharpeners, windows, sinks, and doors.
- Try to provide a quiet space where students can go to avoid stimuli.
- Post simple clear classroom rules in front of the room with eye-catching borders and colors. Also consider posting the desired behaviors and consequences. Cause and effect are ideas that are often lost on ADHD students and logical consequences reinforce the rules.
- Consequences should be delivered consistently and not out of anger or personal frustration.
- Post daily academic schedules and topics in clear sight.

2. Curricular and Teaching Modifications

In the ongoing battle of gaining and maintaining the attention of ADHD students, there are several easy-to-implement modifications an instructor may use:

- Keep curriculum interesting and relevant. Vary the presentation format and relate on-task support materials.

- Use color (pens and chalk), large fonts (handouts), bold lettering, and so on to draw attention to most important aspects of tasks.
- Consider providing guiding outlines or notes to help minimize multi-tasking.
- Make academic tasks brief and give quick feedback.
- Break down tasks to help with organizational difficulties.
- Use proximity and make a habit of positive comments.
- Provide outlets to expend pent-up energy. Bathroom trips or other diversions can help.
- Consider the use of prepackaged curriculum that has been successful for others or that has a research base that supports its effectiveness with ADHD.

3. Peer Intervention

When teachers are attempting to modify the behavior of a student with ADHD, recruiting the aid of classmates as a peer-mediated intervention offers many advantages—including being more efficient in delivering immediate and consistent feedback and promoting generalization across settings—and may result in the improved behavior and academic performance of the peer mediating the intervention.

There are two types of peer interventions. Peers can be used as part of a contingency group. By using peers as contingency groups, peers are given responsibility for general classroom behavior. This can be as a whole class or as groups. Peers can also be used as student leaders or instruments for monitoring and rewarding desirable social and academic behavior. Because of the need for ADHD students to be accepted and the accessibility to immediate feedback, attention improves and impulsivity decreases. Peer tutoring is an instructional strategy in which two students work together on an academic activity with one student providing assistance, instruction, and feedback to the other. During intervention, the students were paired with peer tutors who provided guidance and immediate feedback. Results of this study revealed increased on-task behavior, decreased fidgeting, and increased academic performances on tests (Heward, 2003).

Precautions and Possible Pitfalls

Don't forget to read the current IEP and the student's records for hints and tips. Use it as a starting point. Next seek out the student's case manager for suggestions that might have a successful track record with the individual student. Remember to monitor peer contingency groups for fairness, equity, and a positive tone. Ensure that all group members are participating and disband the group if these factors aren't present.

Sources

Heward, W. L. (2003).Ten faulty notions about teaching and learning that hinder the effectiveness of special education. *Journal of Special Education*. Retrieved December 3, 2004, from www.findarticles.com/p/articles/mi_m0HDF/is_4_36/ai_97116588

McLaughlin, T. F., & Reiber, C. (2004). Classroom interventions: Methods to improve performance and classroom behavior for students with attention-deficit/hyperactivity disorder (ADHD). *International Journal of Special Education, 19*(1), 1–13.

STRATEGY 11: *Practice viewing learning disabilities through the cultural/ethnic eyes of the parents/families of the students.*

What the Research Says

Not all diverse families and cultures view learning disabilities and related educational services the same way. This body of research was supported by a past literature search on cultural issues affecting families with disabilities. With reflection, comments, and recommendations based on a wide range of investigation and thinking on cultural issues surrounding these families, researchers were able to produce a useful paradigm for the understanding of culture in the learning disability service context. Once understanding and a new cultural perspective are facilitated, more effective strategies for interaction with these families can be structured and implemented successfully.

Consideration and research regarding cultural factors and issues affecting families of children with disabilities can be considered recent and relatively new. According to Harry (2002), it should be viewed in the context of the way parental roles have been conceptualized and changed by professionals over the past three decades. Basically, three recent time frames have been defined according to their specific approach.

1. Prior to the 1970s, the emphasis was on psychoanalytic approaches to parents, particularly mothers, an approach that for the most part presented the mother as a victim or patient in severe psychological crisis who needed to go through certain stages of reaction before a point of "acceptance" could be reached. This philosophy focused almost totally on White, middle-class families who could access the kinds of services offered by the psychoanalytic model. While some of the central tenets of that line of thought, such as the notion of

the parent's mourning for an ideal child, seem to be a part of most parents' experience, the literature had two dominant limitations:

    a. the promotion of a pathological view of families of children with disabilities and

    b. a total omission of the impact of differential cultural beliefs and practices on family reactions.

2. The 1970s saw the beginning of the "parent as teacher" approach, which sought to promote and implement positive parental involvement through behavioral training programs. The successes of that approach were reported to be variable, with clear evidence of greater success with middle-class and White families, whose life circumstances, childrearing practices, and personal interaction styles were more consonant with the approaches presented by that model.

3. The advent of P.L. 99–457 in 1986 introduced the current phase, a line of literature that reflects an ideal of the parent as partner or collaborator with professionals. As this ideal evolved into a vision of family-centered practice, issues of diverse family beliefs and practices became a crucial focus (Harry, 2002).

Harry (2002) goes on to describe current trends and influences on cross-cultural issues and cross-cultural professional preparation. The research identified a number of culturally important factors for professionals to consider in preparation for meeting the needs of cross-cultural students who are disabled and their families.

The following section will highlight the principles emerging from the literature on service provision to families who, by virtue of socioeconomic or cultural features, differ significantly from the mainstream. While this information came from Harry (2002), the information was gleaned from a review of the literature that reveals the following six areas of difficulty regarding the provision of culturally appropriate services to families:

1. Cultural differences in definitions and interpretations of disabilities

2. Cultural differences in family coping styles and responses to disability-related stress

3. Cultural differences in parental interaction styles, as well as expectations of participation and advocacy

4. Differential cultural group access to information and services

5. Negative professional attitudes to, and perceptions of, families' roles in the special education process

6. Dissonance in the cultural fit of programs

The challenge of providing culturally appropriate services can be captured by Atkin (1991) reflecting about Black minorities and health and disability services: "Service provision for disabled people usually embodies the views of the provider rather than the user" (p. 45).

Atkin (1991) called for research and service provision policies that are informed by "an account of disability in terms of black people's perceptions without these perceptions being seen as pathological" (p. 46). This principle should be seen as central to the process of decision making about services for minority populations. However, becoming aware and reflecting the "views of the user" is no small goal if teachers essentially do not like, share, or even respect those views.

Application

It is essential to view the son or daughter with a disability through the eyes of a mother or father from highly diverse cultures. In certain settings, there can be subtle but powerful ethnocentrism that makes it difficult for mainstream practitioners or researchers to recognize and give credence to nonmainstream family patterns or practices.

Typically, teachers and other school personnel exhibit mindset differences based on ethnicity or culture. Also, school personnel's strong identification with the culture of educational professionalism can also present a communication barrier, regardless of ethnic identity. Professionals can find it difficult to break the traditional mold of professional monopoly of information and decision making.

Personnel preparation programs for professionals in special education and related fields should include coursework in the study of cross-cultural literature related to families and disabilities. General education teachers should also consider acquiring this type of sensitivity. As more and more special education students are mainstreamed or involved in inclusive programs, these courses should be presented with a strong practical emphasis that requires students to develop and practice an awareness of the cultural principles and concepts on which special education in the United States is based. Consider the following ideas as essential elements of training and preparation in acquiring cross-cultural mastery:

(a) Personal self-examination, reflection and awareness of the cross-cultural paradigm and values clarification/contrasts and comparisons;

(b) Culture-specific knowledge, which includes effective communication techniques;

(c) The ability to apply this knowledge at both appropriate interpersonal and institutional levels;

(d) A posture and style of nonspecific cultural practice and approaches that can lead to successful professional-parent relationships without being totally familiar with the culture or without having specific knowledge;

(e) Use of opportunities to learn from parents and other family members. Consider using family members in roles that support classroom instruction or school related activities. Develop observation and interviewing skills seen through a culturally sensitive lens.

While the focus of this application centers on working with parents of students with disabilities, these suggestions are commonsense suggestions for any educational setting for both special education and general education teachers.

Precautions and Possible Pitfalls

The limitations of a culturally specific approach, however, include the danger of bias and stereotyping and the inability of the elements presented to define the infinite range of differences among cultural groups. Be wary of making decisions that don't reflect the individual student.

Sources

Atkin, K. (1991). Health, illness, disability and Black minorities: A speculative critique of present day discourse. *Disability, Handicap and Society, 6*(1), 37–47.

Glazer, N., & Moynihan, D. P. (1963). *Beyond the melting pot.* Cambridge, MA: MIT Press/Harvard University Press.

Harry, B. (2002). Trends and issues in serving culturally diverse families of children with disabilities. *Journal of Special Education.* Retrieved December 3, 2004, from www.findarticles.com/p/articles/mi_m0HDF/is_3_36/ai_93974001

2

Organizing Lesson Plans for an Effective Learning Environment

The real object of education is to have a man in the condition of continually asking questions.

—Bishop Creighton

 STRATEGY 12: *Develop graphic summaries of student objectives to facilitate the planning for students with special needs.*

What the Research Says

 Although federal laws have moved more and more children with disabilities back into general education classrooms, the results have been somewhat mixed with regard to effective application of the IEP. Researcher Lisa Saint-Laurent (2001) identified that many general education teachers are not familiar with the contents of a student's IEP and so do not use it to help plan their instruction. In order to provide a vehicle to remedy this circumstance, she developed the Summary of Individualized Objectives (SIO). The SIO is a one-page graphic summary of all of the students who have special needs in a given inclusion classroom. The chart is prepared by the special education teacher and is divided into specific academic categories as appropriate (reading, writing, math, study skills, etc.). Under each topic, the specific objectives each student is working on are listed.

The SIO is not just a tool used as a reference in the planning process; it also serves as a communication device between the special education and general education teachers during the consultation process. As evaluation periods occur, the SIO can also be used to facilitate that process, making it an efficient process that can be updated as students meet their objectives.

The SIO is not the only graphic that can be used to facilitate this process. Teachers from a Maryland school district developed a similar approach linking state standards to student IEP objectives. By using a chart to list the standards and then note specific students whose IEP goals addressed those standards, teachers were able to quickly and effectively include those goals in their instructional planning.

Application

In order to facilitate lesson planning, teachers need to take the time to sit down at the start of the year and create a list of their students who have 504 plans or IEPs that have specific accommodations or modifications. Teachers should note important details like the students' learning style and goal area. Depending on the subject area and grade level, teachers should consider designing a suitable chart that allows them to cross-reference the essential standards they are required to teach and the goals the students have.

Some elementary teachers may find it more effective to create a chart that lists the students and the area of need by content area (reading, writing, math, etc.). Other teachers, particularly those who teach single subjects, may find it more effective to create a chart that cross-references the state standards to the students' goal areas.

Whatever the method chosen, teachers should make sure that they update it as students achieve their goals. This chart can be used to track student progress and can be reported to parents at the regular reporting times in addition to the IEP meeting. This kind of charting can be used to benefit all students in a class (see Table 2.1).

Table 2.1   Sample SIO Charts

Elementary Level

Students	Reading	Writing	Math	Study Skills/ Behavior
Jeff	Identify main idea	Use correct spelling	Convert fractions into decimals	Complete tasks on time
Jessica	Read sight words	Produce sentences on topic	Use common denominators	Turn in all assignments
Fred	Increase reading fluency	Write a five-sentence paragraph	Identify math terms in word problems	Use reference materials
Jorge	Use context clues	Put sentences in correct order	Use decimals when working money problems	Raise hand to participate in class

Secondary Level

Students	Goal Area	Accommodations/Modifications
Sabrina	Auditory memory, verbal production of complex sentences	Repeat directions, Books on tape
Geraldo	Track assignments and projects	Extended time on tests
Jon	Reading comprehension	Books on tape
Felicity	Reading and summarizing key elements	Extended time on written assignments

Precautions and Possible Pitfalls

Although it is effective to keep a master list of students with special needs, this information must be kept confidential. Teachers should avoid labeling the list "Special Ed" or something similar, and keep it away from the curious eyes of students and parents. If they use the chart to report on a student's progress, they should cover the parts that are not about that specific student before making the photocopy.

Sources

Saint-Laurent, L. (2001). The SIO: An instrument to facilitate inclusion. *Reading & Writing Quarterly, 17*(4), 349–356.

Walsh, J. M. (2001). Getting the "big picture" of IEP goals and state standards. *Teaching Exceptional Children, 33*(5), 18–27.

STRATEGY 13: Use a "strategy" approach rather than "drill and practice" when teaching math concepts.

What the Research Says

In a study of 84 second graders in which 42 were identified as learning disabled, Tournaki (2003) determined that the success of the students with disabilities was dependent on the type of math instruction they received. The study created three groups of students. The first received pullout instruction in math facts using drill and practice. The second group received pullout instruction using a strategy approach. The third group acted as a control and received no pullout instruction. Although nondisabled students improved with both kinds of instructional pullout, the students with special needs improved their math skills when taught math strategies rather than direct instruction with drill and practice. When asked to respond to math questions requiring a transfer of math skill, only the strategy group improved their performance.

Application

Often teachers perceive that the acquisition of math facts is facilitated by drill and practice. Repetition and speed drills are commonly employed to build mastery. These exercises are often painful and frustrating for the student with a learning disability. Taking the time to teach the strategy behind the math fact may yield a more positive outcome in the long run. Consider a guided instructional delivery where the class moves together through the specific strategy. Students are then given a variety of problems to apply the strategy to. The strategy can be retaught as needed to ensure student success.

This approach is supportive of a constructivist view of math that is endorsed by the National Math Standards. More and more, students are being asked to explain their answers in math assessments as well as provide the correct solution. Beginning that dialogue with a teacher's support, the student can explore a strategy and how it can be applied in a variety of situations. This will help the student develop the logical thinking skills that are essential to higher-level math—algebra and geometry.

Some teachers will take this a step further and invite their students to create their own math questions. Students will then present their questions to each other and explain how to use the strategy to find the correct answer. Student-generated examples don't have the "neat" answers that math textbooks do and may help students become less intimidated about applying math in a variety of settings.

Precautions and Possible Pitfalls

 It is important that teachers recognize that some students may never progress to the automaticity levels that their nondisabled peers achieve. Regardless of lack of speed, the advantage for the student with a disability is that, having learned the strategy, he or she will have the opportunity to approach unfamiliar problems with the strategy in mind.

Source

Tournaki, N. (2003). The differential effects of teaching addition through strategy instruction versus drill and practice to students with and without learning disabilities. *Journal of Learning Disabilities, 36*(5), 449–459.

 STRATEGY 14: *Incorporate the nine principles of Universal Design for Learning when creating instructional plans.*

What the Research Says

Just as Universal Design in architecture allows the builder to incorporate design principles that benefit a wide range of people while saving the expense of retrofitting an older building, Universal Design for Learning allows an instructor to create a lesson that meets the broad range of student needs. Scott, McGuire, and Shaw (2003) noted that college instruction differs from K–12 instruction in three main areas: legal mandates regarding access, specification of curriculum, and preparation of instructors. This research reviewed the changes in postsecondary education over the past decades and traced the origin and development of Universal Design for Learning (UDL). Changing demographics require changes in postsecondary instructional practices. The July 2000 American Council on Education reported that two-thirds of at-risk students go on to college, and many of these students qualify for special education services through Section 504 and ADA. Most typically, these students are given accommodations based on their disabilities (extended time, note-taker, etc.). Changes in the student population have occurred simultaneously with changes in technology, professorships, and the idea that the student is a consumer.

From this starting point, Scott et al. (2003) extensively reviewed the literature on Universal Design and identified nine basic principles that can be implemented at any level:

1. Equitable use. Instruction is designed to be accessible to students with diverse abilities.

2. Flexibility in use. Multimodal instruction provides for student choice.

3. Simple and intuitive. Instruction is designed in a predictable manner with unnecessary complexity eliminated.

4. Perceptible information. Instruction is communicated effectively to each student regardless of student's sensory abilities.

5. Tolerance for error. Instruction anticipates variations in student pace and skills.

6. Low physical effort. Minimize nonessential physical effort.

7. Size and space appropriate for use. Instruction considers student's body size, posture, mobility, and communication needs.

8. A community of learners. Instruction promotes interaction and communication between students.

9. Instructional climate. The climate is welcoming and inclusive with high expectations for all students.

Application

Although this body of research focused on postsecondary instructional practice, the nine principles identified are essential elements of quality instruction at any level. In K–12 teaching, it can be easy to rely on what teachers are told to do—"Teach the adopted text, give extended time because the IEP says to," and so on. Yet the difference between an adequate teacher and an excellent teacher has always been and will always be the ability to inspire significant learning in his or her students. By considering the nine elements of Universal Design for Learning, teachers can endemically create a classroom environment that supports all students.

Consider the idea of equitable use. With the availability of technology increasing, teachers can provide copies of lecture notes and homework assignments online for ease of student access where assistive technology can be utilized by students with diverse needs. This ties in to the second element, flexibility in use. Most teachers know that variety in instruction (group work, labs, lecture, video, skits, etc.) enhances student interest, but adding student choice into assignments encourages students to learn the way they learn best.

Keeping material simple and intuitive seems obvious, yet many students can't make the connections that their classmates do. By providing clear and written explanation, rubrics, and expectations for assignments, teachers can eliminate many points of confusion for their students. In keeping with this is the idea that the information should be perceptible to the students. Teachers need to consider how students are able to communicate (e.g., in another language, with a hearing aid, with Braille, etc.) and design instruction that is accessible for all students.

Tolerance for error implies that teachers recognize and accept the fact that their students have different skill levels. Teachers can support students by building in opportunities for skill development (practice) and feedback on a regular basis. By allowing students to turn in parts of larger projects as they go along, teachers can ensure that students are progressing appropriately.

The idea of low physical effort invites teachers to understand that some students have physical limitations that may impede their progress. For example, some students are unable to handwrite at length and may be more successful with a word processor. This concept dovetails with the idea of size and space. Students come in all shapes and sizes, and teachers need to be cognizant of the needs of their students. Many desks are too small for the suddenly tall adolescent and completely inaccessible for a student in a wheelchair. Even classroom design can influence student success. Some students thrive in small groups; others benefit from linear rows to help focus their attention. Teachers should keep these needs in mind as they design their instruction to facilitate the growth of a community of learners. By encouraging students to work together and maintain ongoing dialogue about the content, teachers can facilitate student communication and learning. Many teachers encourage students to use chat rooms or Instant Messenger to set up study sessions to keep the communication going.

All of these concepts come together to create an effective instructional climate that emphasizes respect and diversity. Teachers can reiterate the importance of attitude through activities, modeling, and discussion.

Precautions and Pitfalls

At first, implementing all nine elements in instructional design to create a universally accessible curriculum may seem daunting. Yet the secret to effective implementation lies in awareness and adaptability over time. Teachers need to realize that small steps add up over time, and creating a Universal Design is an ongoing process based in reflection, student achievement, and feedback.

Source

Scott, S. S., McGuire, J. M., & Shaw, S. F. (2003). Universal design for instruction. *Remedial & Special Education, 24*(6), 369–380.

STRATEGY 15: *Tap the strengths of students with attention deficit/hyperactivity disorder (ADHD) with effective instructional strategies.*

What the Research Says

In a recent study (Zentall, Hall, & Grskovic, 2001), researchers reported that the most effective instructional strategies for students with ADHD were those that included personal attention, opportunities to be in leadership or helper roles, and the use of preferred activities as incentives. The least effective instructional strategies were those that took away or withheld a preferred activity.

Application

Stimulation through social interactions and activity-based lessons have been found to be effective with students with special needs. Teachers should avoid lengthy doses of seat time and sedentary work. The use of hands-on and manipulative activities is also more effective with students with disabilities and may enable them to be successful. Providing the student with opportunities to move around the classroom can also be helpful. Allowing the student to run an errand, hand out papers, clean the board, or help out in the classroom can help reinforce appropriate behavior.

Because students with ADHD may experience greater difficulty in starting and organizing tasks, the teacher should consider breaking assignments down into smaller pieces while remembering to check for understanding at regular intervals. Chunking curriculum is a strategy that benefits all students, not just those with disabilities.

Students with ADHD can be a real pleasure to have in class. These students have an energy and enthusiasm that, when harnessed, can create the most dynamic of lessons. These are the students who will volunteer for kinesthetic activities like role playing, skits, mock trials, and so on. They will ask questions that stimulate class discussion and often enjoy debate.

Teachers should consider the classroom environment and how it supports or interferes with the needs of a student with ADHD. For example, a classroom near a heavy student traffic area (drinking fountain, restroom, etc.) may prove to be very distracting for the student and he or she may require preferential seating to help minimize the distraction. Conversely, a classroom that is designed for student movement and group activities is an ideal setting for a student with ADHD.

For a teacher working with a student with ADHD, the first person to seek out for support can be a veteran special education teacher who has a thorough understanding of the student's IEP. Using a special education teacher to help plan activities and lessons can be a tremendous resource. He or she can also provide helpful hints in dealing with discipline issues, preferential seating, and the importance of presenting clear, specific, and simple directions.

Precautions and Possible Pitfalls

It is a common mistake to try to modify the negative behaviors of a student with ADHD by restricting participation and withholding privileges. These approaches may seem reasonable in the short term but ironically contribute to an increase in negative behavior rather than a decrease. Teachers need to be wary of the punitive aspects of their management systems and try to frame consequences in a positive light. For example, rather than keeping a student with ADHD in at recess, a teacher may choose to reward positive behavior with a first-in-line pass. If the teacher is organized and has straightforward and concise classroom rules and procedures with consequences clearly stated, the chances for student success increase.

Source

Zentall, S. S., Hall, A. M., & Grskovic, J. A. (2001). Learning and motivational characteristics of boys with AD/HD and/or giftedness. *Exceptional Children, 67*(4), 419–519.

 STRATEGY 16: Remember that less = more and streamline the content of the curriculum.

What the Research Says

 Eylon and Linn (1988) report that, cognitively, students respond better to a systematic, in-depth treatment of a few topics than they do to conventional in-breadth treatment of many topics. Increasingly, it is recommended that teachers of all subjects stream-line the curriculum and focus more on a limited set of knowledge and skills. Students' misconceptions and lack of understanding of basics reflect limitations of mental processing and memory. Ted Sizer, a well-known progressive educator, identifies "less is more" as one of the major princi-ples to guide educational reform (cited in Cushman, 1994).

Application

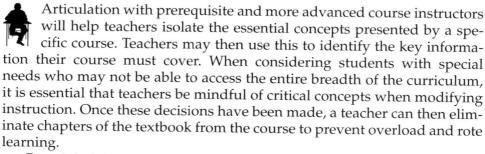 Articulation with prerequisite and more advanced course instructors will help teachers isolate the essential concepts presented by a spe-cific course. Teachers may then use this to identify the key informa-tion their course must cover. When considering students with special needs who may not be able to access the entire breadth of the curriculum, it is essential that teachers be mindful of critical concepts when modifying instruction. Once these decisions have been made, a teacher can then elim-inate chapters of the textbook from the course to prevent overload and rote learning.

By minimizing extraneous detail, teachers can encourage students to focus on the depth of specific concepts and their application to a variety of settings. For example, understanding the classification structure and how different organisms are related through characteristics will better prepare students for hands-on observation than memorizing a variety of worm types.

Precautions and Possible Pitfalls

With today's emphasis on standards-based instruction and high-stakes assessment, teachers should be careful to ensure their cur-riculum meets the requirements outlined by the state. In addition, however, teachers shouldn't automatically throw out "diamonds in the rough," potentially interesting learning pathways, or favorite topics. There's a lot to be said for the effects of teacher enthusiasm for specific concepts, topics, and content on student motivation. A wise teacher will use them!

Sources

Cushman, K. (1994, November). Less is more: The secret of being essential. *Horace,* *11*(2), 1–4. Available at www.essentialschools.org

Eylon, B., & Linn, M. (1988). Learning and instruction: An examination of four research perspectives in science education. *Review of Educational Research, 58,* 251–301.

STRATEGY 17: Encourage students to take advantage of out-of-school learning opportunities.

What the Research Says

 Learning outside of school (informal education) plays a vital role in the development of competence in language, reading, mathematics, and a variety of other school-related domains. Assume that such learning also contributes to classroom learning, motivation, and attitude. Informal learning experiences help preschool children acquire a wide range of early literacy before the children enter school. They learn a language, usually before entering any formal classroom!

Korpan, Bisanz, Bisanz, Boehme, and Lynch (1997) conducted structured interviews of parents with elementary school children that revealed the nature and scope of children's science-related activities outside of school. Their research exposed a remarkable level of participation in extracurricular, science-related activities. Categories of participation included both nonfiction and science fiction television shows as well as reading activities, computer use, community activities such as zoos, home observations and simple science experiments, questioning and discussion, and household interest and familiarity with science. Often, time and interaction with science-related activities outside the formal science classroom exceeds time in the classroom.

While this study of informal learning looked primarily at science activities, it would come as no surprise to find the same sort of informal connections to the other disciplines.

Application

The studies make it clear that learning outside of school should not be ignored and can be a new source of motivating instructional strategies, particularly for students with special needs. If students are required to spend only a few hours a week in science instruction, the overall role schooling plays in developing science literacy is questionable. The influence of home and community environments needs to become a factor in planning more formalized content instruction for students who may need more time or greater exposure to scientific concepts.

Simple structured interviews or questionnaires can yield insights and characterize the development of content thinking from outside the school boundaries. This knowledge can yield a perspective on common experiences (e.g., exhibits at a museum) that can facilitate discussions, interpret phenomena, and frame classroom lessons and activities. Information could also serve to highlight a range of motivations and competencies among students and help teachers identify areas in which student "experts" could make a contribution to classroom learning, content projects, or other activities. It also can help identify influential allies at home who can reinforce teacher efforts with individual students or act as a broader class resource.

There is a full range of informal content-related activities students bring to class. While this informal activity or exploration may diminish or change as students get older, much of their background and attitudes are based on this informal education. It may also become more specialized as a student finds some disciplines more interesting than others.

Students with disabilities characterized by a high incidence of perseveration may prove to be an inexhaustible resource on specific content. For example, a seventh-grade student diagnosed with Asperger Syndrome knew every scientific name for every dinosaur as well as every characteristic, including the relevant geological periods, and proved to be an even greater resource for the class assignment than many of the materials from the library.

By remaining cognizant of the influence home and community environments have on overall content literacy, teachers can begin to incorporate the information into their instructional practices. Creative teachers can explore, enhance, and develop a range of curricular connections to the students' informal background.

Precautions and Possible Pitfalls

School learning is often seen in a less enjoyable and sometimes more threatening light than the informal learning students encounter outside of the classroom. Much of the students' experience outside the classroom can be classified as "edutainment." Integrating the two realms is a challenging but very doable task. Research into the connections is just beginning to illuminate instructional relationships and doesn't yet offer a wide range of tested curricula to use the knowledge. Create strategies to integrate the two paradigms within instructional objectives and comfort zones.

Using resources outside the classroom can be a source of inequity due to access problems. Not all students have supportive parents or parents who can provide resources. If credit will be offered to students who are asked to use resources outside of the classroom, offer a classroom or school-based option to those who can't participate off campus.

Sources

Korpan, C. A., Bisanz, G. L., Bisanz, J., Boehme, C., & Lynch, M. A. (1997). What did you learn outside of school today? Using structured interviews to document home and community activities related to science and technology. *Science Education, 81*(6), 651–662.

Ramsey-Gassert, L. (1997). Learning science beyond the classroom. *Elementary School Journal, 97*(4), 95–113.

 STRATEGY 18: *Implement Universal Design principles when teaching science.*

What the Research Says

 Bredderman (1982) examined the common design approaches to science instruction at the elementary level. He noted that science curriculum, by its nature, tends to be vocabulary focused and often textbook driven as a result. This presents a significant obstacle for students with literacy deficits. In spite of research conducted in the early 1980s that concluded that hands-on approaches actually yield better student performance than textbook-driven courses (Bredderman, 1982), many science programs center on the textbook.

Bredderman (1982) found that the most common model in elementary education is the spiral curriculum, which addresses about 15 general science topics and repeats these topics each year. The model is textbook based and allows for little deviation from the text. The second model he identified was the intensified curriculum, in which more time is spent on one or two modules. This model lends itself to adaptation for students with diverse needs. The third model identified was the integrated curriculum model, in which two or more concept bases are brought together (e.g., math and science). Lastly, the theme-based model unifies concepts, which are used to cross topics (e.g., energy, liquids, etc.).

Each of these models has elements that have value for students learning science, but the researchers believe that the greatest success can be obtained from a multiple-option curriculum like Science for All Children (SAC). SAC was developed by 10 general and special education teachers in Buffalo and 22 general and special education teachers in New Orleans. The vital elements of SAC are those of Universal Design. All teachers have access to all materials for all grades; there are multiple means of expression; there are no significant demands for reading proficiency; and there are unlimited material formats and supplemental activities that can be included. SAC invites students to develop science literacy along with reading literacy.

Application

 Although teachers may not have access to Science for All Children materials, the same elements can be incorporated into any science classroom. By varying both input (instruction) and output (activities and assignments), teachers can create a curriculum that supports the learning of all students. Simple ideas like preparing flexible worksheets where some students fill in blanks while others summarize information from a physics text allow for a wide range of literacy skills levels.

Similarly, group work can be organized into tasks that require the use of scientific problem solving at a variety of levels. Students can apply skills like identifying analogies, detecting absurdities, divergent thinking, and finding causes as they use the scientific processes of classification, calibration, observation, and data collection. Group tasks can be structured to be adaptable to each student's abilities.

It is important to design instruction that aligns with expected outcomes. For example, if the lesson goal is to define specific vocabulary, then instruction should facilitate memory and mastery of those terms. If the goal is to use scientific processes like observation and data collection, then teachers must ensure their students have the opportunity to practice these skills.

Precautions and Possible Pitfalls

Although this research specifically addresses science instruction, the concepts behind the instructional design are applicable to any content area. When teachers take the time to design curriculum that is accessible to a wide range of students, all students benefit. By ensuring that instruction includes multiple means of representation, multiple means of expression, and multiple means of engagement, the learning of all students is facilitated.

Sources

Bredderman, T. (1982). The effects of activity-based science in elementary schools. In M. B. Rowe (Ed.), *Education in the 80's: Science* (pp. 63–75). Washington, DC: National Education Association.

Cawley, J. F., Foley, T. E., & Miller, J. (2003). Science and students with mild disabilities. *Intervention in School & Clinic, 38*(3), 160–182.

 STRATEGY 19: Establish scaffolds to help students as they learn complex skills and procedures.

What the Research Says

Walberg (1991) suggests that in science it is especially useful for students to struggle with interesting, meaningful problems that can stimulate discussion about competing approaches.

This idea can be stretched to include all disciplines. He recommends using what he calls comprehension teaching, more commonly called scaffolding, which involves providing students with temporary support until they can perform tasks on their own. Based on Vygotsky's (1978) concept of the "zone of proximal development," teachers build from what students can do with temporary guidance from a more competent person, gradually reducing and eventually removing this support as students become independent thinkers and learners who can perform the task or use the skill on their own. The zone of proximal development refers to the area within which the student can receive support from another to successfully perform a task that he or she cannot perform independently. Scaffolding has been found to be an excellent method of developing students' higher-level thinking skills (Rosenshine & Meister, 1992). Scaffolding is a strategy for gradually and systematically shifting responsibility and control over learning and performance from the teacher to the student.

Application

Through a variety of methods (e.g., observation, listening, tests), assess students' abilities to perform and not perform important skills or tasks independently. Test their ability to perform or not perform these skills or tasks with assistance from another in order to conceptualize their zones of proximal development. Teachers can use a scaffolding approach for skills and tasks that are within the students' zones. Scaffolds can range from a simple hint, clue, example, or question to a complex sequence of activities that begin with teacher-centered approaches (e.g., explaining, demonstrating) but end as student-centered (e.g., self-questioning, self-monitoring).

The example that follows is a scaffolding approach for teaching students to construct graphic organizers of text they have read. It is a complex sequence of steps that uses scaffolding to shift from teacher direction and control of creating graphic organizers to student self-direction and self-control over making them.

1. Show and explain a variety of traditional examples of graphic organizers, such as flow charts, concept maps, and matrices, made by both professionals and students.

2. Inform students about what graphic organizers are and when, why, and how to use various types of them. Jones, Pierce, and Hunter (1988/1989) provide information on why and how to create graphic organizers to comprehend text, and they provide illustrations of a spider map, a continuum or scale, a series of events chain, a compare-contrast matrix, a problem-solution outline, a network tree, a fishbone map, a human-interaction outline, and a cycle. Novak (1998) focuses on concept maps and Vee diagrams.

3. As class work or a homework assignment, give students a partially completed graphic organizer to finish on their own. Give students feedback on their completions. For students of different abilities, a variety of graphic organizers can be used. For the more capable student, a larger number of spaces are required; for the less capable student, fewer blanks or less complex responses may be acceptable.

4. Assign class work or homework that requires students to complete an empty graphic organizer structure entirely on their own. Give students feedback. For students with disabilities, consider allowing them to work with a partner prior to completing the assignment on their own.

5. Assign class work or homework requiring groups of students to create their own graphic organizers. Teachers should assign the groups heterogeneously, paying close attention to personality as well as abilities. Give students specific criteria or rubrics for constructing and evaluating graphic organizers. Criteria may include (a) neat and easy to read; (b) ideas are expressed clearly; (c) ideas are expressed completely but succinctly; (d) content is organized clearly and logically; (e) labels or other strategies (colors, lines) are used to guide the reader's comprehension; (f) main ideas, not minor details, are emphasized; (g) it is visually appealing; and (h) the reader doesn't have to turn the page to read the words.

6. Once their graphic organizers are completed, the groups show their graphic organizers to the other groups, who critique the graphic organizers and give them feedback based on the criteria identified above. Teachers should supplement the feedback as needed.

7. For homework, students develop graphic organizers completely on their own, using the identified criteria. Group members give each other homework feedback on the extent to which they met the established criteria.

8. Finally, students are expected to be able to create and critique their own graphic organizers and support from others (students and teacher) isn't needed.

Precautions and Possible Pitfalls

To use scaffolding effectively, it is vital for teachers to consider issues such as: what types of support to provide and when, what order to sequence them in, and criteria for deciding when it is time to reduce or withdraw support from students. It is also very important to make sure scaffolding attempts are truly within the students' zone of proximal development. If they are below this area, activities will be too easy because the student can really do them independently. If they are above this area, no amount of scaffolding will enable students to perform independently because the skill or task is too difficult given the students' prior knowledge or skills.

Sources

Jones, B. F., Pierce, J., & Hunter, B. (1988/1989). Teaching students to construct graphic representations. *Educational Leadership,* 20–25.

Novak, J. (1998). *Learning, creating and using knowledge: Concept maps as facilitative tools in schools and corporations.* Mahwah, NJ: Erlbaum.

Rosenshine, B., & Meister, C. (1992). The use of scaffolds for teaching higher-level cognitive strategies. *Educational Leadership, 49*(7), 26–34.

Vygotsky, L. S. (1978). *Mind in society: The development of higher psychological processes.* Cambridge, MA: Harvard University Press.

Walberg, H. (1991). Improving school science in advanced and developing countries. *Review of Educational Research, 61*(1), 25–69.

STRATEGY 20: *Fight boredom by using classroom strategies that stimulate student interest.*

What the Research Says

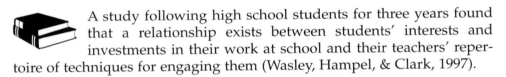

A study following high school students for three years found that a relationship exists between students' interests and investments in their work at school and their teachers' repertoire of techniques for engaging them (Wasley, Hampel, & Clark, 1997).

Application

Although each new school year brings enthusiasm and optimism for students and teachers, once students encounter instructional routines and procedures that become predictable, their enthusiasm for learning may begin to wane. This is particularly true for students with short attention spans.

By using a range of instructional strategies from one unit to the next, student interest is stimulated. For example, a teacher might have students listen to a speech, discuss it in a group, and then write a paper about the speech. Following this project, the teacher may have students do a group assignment about favorite speeches and the people who gave them. Students could finish up this unit by either delivering their favorite speech or writing one of their own. The instructional model of reading the book, answering the questions at the end of the chapter, listening to a lecture or watching a video, and taking a test does not provide for good instruction. There is no research to support that this method is effective.

Offering a variety of instructional strategies is not only stimulating for teachers and students alike, but addresses more fully the diverse needs of all students. Most teachers are aware of the characteristics of different learning styles and multiple intelligence theory and can incorporate that knowledge into creative and effective instructional practice.

Essential to the success of varying instructional strategies is support from school districts in providing professional growth opportunities for teachers by encouraging them to attend workshops or seminars or to network with colleagues about best teaching practices. Also of critical importance is the reflection by the teacher after a lesson is taught. Another powerful strategy is to invite observation by fellow colleagues or mentors. An observation of a teacher's lesson and the reflective conversation afterward can be a "mirror" to the teacher of what is really going on in the classroom. These observations can help teachers understand that mirroring is essential to their development as professionals.

In many teacher induction programs around the country, districts are now focusing on helping new teachers build a repertoire of techniques, skills, and strategies through ongoing professional development. Districts must allow time for new teachers to attend seminars, conferences, and observations of exemplary teachers to assist these emerging teachers in building a repertoire that is responsive to the students they serve.

Precautions and Possible Pitfalls

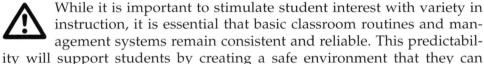 While it is important to stimulate student interest with variety in instruction, it is essential that basic classroom routines and management systems remain consistent and reliable. This predictability will support students by creating a safe environment that they can count on. This is particularly important for students with specific disabilities (autism, Asperger Syndrome, developmental delays, etc.), who are negatively affected by change.

Teachers sometimes fall into a pattern of using a particular strategy (especially if it has been successful) to the detriment of any others. Although it is important for teachers to take risks in the classroom, it is just as important to learn what works and what doesn't in a particular classroom setting. Students like consistency and routine to a point; however, if the instructional strategies are never varied, the students become bored and disinterested. Do not be afraid to consult with other teachers on ways to vary strategies, whether it is on the type of assessment being used or using Socratic dialogue to generate student opinions on a piece of literature. It is important to remember that no one technique or strategy works every time with every student.

Source

Wasley, P., Hampel, R., & Clark, R. (1997). *Kids and school reform.* San Francisco: Jossey-Bass.

STRATEGY 21: Increase the effectiveness of homework as a learning tool for students with disabilities by using research-tested strategies and accommodations.

What the Research Says

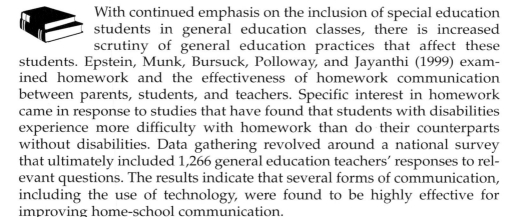

With continued emphasis on the inclusion of special education students in general education classes, there is increased scrutiny of general education practices that affect these students. Epstein, Munk, Bursuck, Polloway, and Jayanthi (1999) examined homework and the effectiveness of homework communication between parents, students, and teachers. Specific interest in homework came in response to studies that have found that students with disabilities experience more difficulty with homework than do their counterparts without disabilities. Data gathering revolved around a national survey that ultimately included 1,266 general education teachers' responses to relevant questions. The results indicate that several forms of communication, including the use of technology, were found to be highly effective for improving home-school communication.

Teachers need to be cognizant of the idea that students with learning disabilities—and sometimes others—may need accommodations in the way homework is organized and structured as a learning device. In addition, parents and the home environment must be active considerations in a successful homework policy.

When students leave class, the teaching and learning environment for doing schoolwork becomes unequal. All students are going home and into their communities to a variety of environments and relationships that are different in many respects. In one home, a student might be supported by college-educated parents, reference resources, Internet, and a quiet work place. In another home, a parent works nights at two jobs and there are few resources available. The opportunity to overcome or compensate for a disability in one environment may be optimal and nonexistent in another environment. Is it fair? No, but it is reality for many students once they leave the classroom. This means homework needs to be well thought out and structured carefully so as not to put any student at a disadvantage.

The results of the Epstein et al. (1999) research indicated that general education teachers perceived several common practices, as well as use of technology, to be highly effective for improving home-school communication about homework for students with disabilities. Among the most highly ranked recommendations were release and mutual planning time, assignment books and logs, parent attendance at meetings and daily monitoring of their child's homework, and use of telephone networks or answering machines to provide remote access to assignments. To this list and beyond the research we can add Web sites and group e-mailing, as teachers reach out for greater communication. Each method comes with its own strengths and limitations and would need to be considered on a site-by-site and teacher-by-teacher basis. What follows is a summary of the research findings and a list of suggestions and possible considerations within the homework paradigm. While there were other research outcomes for each category and question about homework practices, only the top few are presented here:

General Educators' Efforts to Communicate With Parents and Students
1. General education teachers should require that students keep a daily assignment book.
2. At the start of school, general education teachers should provide parents with a list of suggestions on how parents can assist with homework.
3. General education teachers should remind students of due dates on a regular basis.

Adapting Policies to Facilitate Communication
1. Schools should provide incentives for teachers who engage in specific activities to improve home-school communication.
2. Schools should schedule parent-teacher conferences in the evenings for working parents.
3. Schools should provide release time for teachers to communicate with parents.

Increased Student Responsibility
1. Students should keep a daily assignment book.
2. Students should ask the teacher for help if they do not understand an assignment.
3. Students should learn how to manage their time more effectively.

General and Special Education Communication
1. General and special education teachers should share information regarding homework adaptations that are effective for students with disabilities.
2. Special education teachers should provide general education teachers with information about the strengths and weaknesses of students with disabilities.

3. General education and special education teachers should share a common planning period during the school day.

Technologies to Enhance Communication

1. Schools should establish systems that enable teachers to place homework assignments on audiotapes so that parents can access the assignments by telephone or voice mail.
2. Schools should use answering machines so that parents can leave messages for teachers at any time.
3. Schools should provide e-mail for teachers so that they can send assignments to the home electronically.
4. Schools should establish telephone network hotlines so that parents can call when questions or problems arise over homework assignments.
5. Schools should regularly provide computerized student progress reports for parents.

Application

Homework is one aspect of the general education curriculum that has been widely recognized as important to academic success. Teachers have long used homework to provide additional learning time, strengthen study and organizational skills, and in some respects, keep parents informed of their children's progress. Generally, when students with disabilities participate in the general education curriculum, they are expected to complete homework along with their peers. But, just as students with disabilities may need instructional accommodations in the classroom, they may also need homework accommodations.

Many students with disabilities and their parents find homework challenging, and teachers are frequently called upon to make accommodations for these students. It is essential that teachers work as carefully on homework strategies as they do on other parts of the curriculum.

Teachers should make sure students and parents have information regarding the policy on missed and late assignments, extra credit, and available adaptations. Some homework tips for teachers:

- Consider creating an established homework routine. It helps.
- Make sure the homework is doable for all stakeholders.
- Explain all assignments carefully and allow time for feedback.
- Write the assignment on the board for more visual learners.
- Use verbal reminders.
- Coordinate with other teachers to avoid overload.
- Have the homework realistically connect and interface with classroom curriculum.

- Try to relate homework to relevant real-life situations if possible (or inform students how they will use the content of the homework in real life).
- If necessary, explain how to do the homework, provide examples, and write directions on the board.
- Start homework in class if it needs to be supported with direct help.

Teachers should consider individual homework accommodations and make any necessary modifications to the homework assignment before sending it home. Survey other special education teachers and general education teachers to identify practices that will be most helpful to individual students. The most common homework accommodations are to

- Connect directly with those who need it
- Monitor more closely if needed
- Allow alternative outcomes or customize the assignment
- Provide learning tools to those who are not likely to have them
- Provide a peer tutor or assign the student to a study group
- Adjust time frames
- Adjust evaluation standards, if needed

It is important to involve others in all accommodations. What has worked before for this student? If teachers, students, or families do not find homework accommodations reasonable or useful, they may not use them.

Teachers should also teach homework strategies and skills. Many students, particularly those with learning disabilities, need instruction in study and organizational skills. Here is a list of organizational strategies basic to homework:

- Include strategies for parents, with suggestions and policies, right from the beginning of the class.
- Help students explore the wide range of homework strategies available and help them find out which homework strategies work best for them.
- Find ways to facilitate peer tutoring arrangements and involve parents.
- Make sure all needed materials are available and organized for class consumption.
- Help students break down assignments and develop a sequential plan for completing multitask assignments.
- Treat the assessment and evaluation of homework as an important part of the learning environment. Consider pregrading or checking assignments for accuracy and completion and offer revision opportunities before turning them in.

- Create a homework "rubric" and consider some credit for work completed on time in addition to the content credit.
- Teachers should teach students to "learn to learn."
- Teach and give credit for students successfully organizing their homework and study time beyond the class content. Notebooks, calendars, and other strategies may not connect directly to the content, but teaching students how to learn or "learning to learn" is a worthy goal for all students at any age.

Teachers should also ensure clear home-school communication. Recommended ways that teachers can improve communications with parents include:

- Encourage students to keep assignment books.
- Form e-mail group mailing lists for those who might use them.
- Have an outgoing message machine for parents to call.
- Use Web pages for projects and larger assignments that are known about ahead of time.
- Provide a list of suggestions on how parents might assist with homework. Hand it out in paper form and post it on a Web page.
- Share information with other teachers regarding student strengths and needs and necessary accommodations.

Remember, schools are competing with friends, afterschool activities (that may be sanctioned by parents), and a huge range of other distractions that students will prioritize in addition to their homework. Sometimes even parents feel ballet or a soccer game is more important than homework. Making homework doable and user-friendly and offering suitable rewards helps tip their decisions, making teacher efforts and planning worthwhile.

Precautions and Possible Pitfalls

Even with the most careful planning, organization, and student training, a teacher can only control the homework environment to a point. This means there may be inequities that can't be compensated for, no matter what. There are some schools and individuals who have given up trying to get students to engage in homework. There could be many reasons for this, but inertia continues to pressure students not to do homework. If students don't feel homework is important to them or meaningful, it may take some time, creative effort, and planning to change the climate. It may also take a department or schoolwide effort to accomplish this.

Source

Epstein, M. H., Munk, D. D., Bursuck, W. D., Polloway, E. A., Jayanthi, M. (1999). Strategies for improving home-school communication about homework for students with disabilities. *Journal of Special Education, 33*(3), 166.

STRATEGY 22: Be aware of the common problems and changes in instructional strategies associated with a switch to block scheduling for all students.

What the Research Says

Reacting to concerns about the traditional six-period high school schedule, many alternative scheduling patterns have evolved from the general paradigm called "block scheduling." They are called a variety of names: "intensive block," "4x4 block," "A/B plan," or "modified block," but share the quality of reducing the number of classes offered during a school day. According to the researchers, schools that have restructured their school day using some form of the block schedule have reaped many benefits including increased school achievement, improved critical thinking skills, enhanced school climate, more collaborative learning and teaching practices, increased opportunities for curriculum enhancement, and more active, student-initiated learning.

Using quantitative research to examine the impact of a block schedule on an inclusive high school program that had been functioning for a number of years, McLeskey and Weller (2000) identified themes related to benefits and challenges of block scheduling and the inclusion of students labeled with high-incidence disabilities. The results of this study show that inclusion and block scheduling were complementary and mutually supportive aspects of school reform in the targeted high school. While McLeskey and Weller identified several challenges related to block scheduling, they believed none of the challenges were unique to students with disabilities.

Application

Most educational professionals see the change to block scheduling as also a change from a teacher-centered instructional style to a more student-centered instructional style. Students are expected to be engaged in a more proactive pathway toward orchestrated self-directed learning. Sometimes called problem-based or discovery learning, this style is a move away from the teacher-centered lecture format. More group work and active student learning is expected. Students more familiar with the teacher-centered approach will need to be supported in the change. They may feel their grades or status as students is threatened.

The following issues were the major challenges McLeskey and Weller (2000) identified:

1. There was a magnified need for both teachers and students to develop effective organizational skills. In some models, students and teachers have different classes, different subjects, and different teachers and students every day. Students may have trouble keeping track of books, assignments, due dates, and quizzes and exams. There may be a steeper learning curve for students with disabilities adapting to the block schedule, but this becomes less of an issue as experience increases.

2. Student absences are a huge issue in a block schedule. Missing a day or two of classes means they've missed a whole week of instruction. The consequences of absences are magnified because of the increased pace of instruction and the fact that some block schedules run alternate days. Teachers will need to develop strategies to help students who have trouble coping with the greater time frames. Teachers will need to be more proactive in helping students with protocols for making up missed classes.

3. Often students will say, "I cannot sit this long" or "I can't be quiet this long." For some students, the block is too long despite the use of block-friendly, student-centered strategies. Sometimes a simple trip to the restroom helps solve these problems. Changing activities from a quiet seat-based instructional strategy to a more active mode helps. Each class will be different based on the student mix.

According to the research, overall, inclusion worked well within block scheduling strategies and didn't seem to be detrimental for students with disabilities. In fact, block scheduling contributed a more supportive, learner-centered program. Prepared teachers could easily address the three major issues discussed here.

Precautions and Possible Pitfalls

Absences can be a big problem in some communities and become the greatest threat to a student's standing in classes. They are also a major source of parental complaints and intervention. There is nothing more frustrating to a teacher than families who take students away on vacations, ski trips, and so on. They miss tests and due dates, and because their parents sanction the missed days, often students feel they bear little responsibility. Be proactive. It is suggested that teachers include school policy and class policy in the course syllabus for absences and make-up work. The policy should cover protocols for these absence-based dilemmas. Teachers should run them past school officials for support and make students and parents aware of them. It may not prevent all problems associated with absences, but it helps.

Source

McLeskey, J., & Weller, D. R. (2000). Block scheduling and inclusion in a high school. *Remedial and Special Education, 21*(4), 209.

3

Using Formal, Informal, and Alternative Student Assessment

The kids in our classroom are infinitely more significant than the subject we're teaching them.

—Meladee McCarty

 STRATEGY 23: When grading student writing, consider what the student is able to do well before noting what needs improvement.

What the Research Says

 In a review of current research, Gregg and Mather (2002) noted that there are many factors that influence the perception that a student is not a proficient writer. They propose that by considering writing skills (spelling, syntax, vocabulary, etc.) as well as the task format (dictating, copying, timed writing, etc.), teachers will discover a student's writing strengths and will also notice areas that require support. They note that it is vital to remember that writing is integrally related to social interactions and dialogue. In other words, writing is not simply the attempt to represent linguistic structures such as sentences, words, or phonemes; written expression requires a social process achieved through dialogue and interaction.

Application

 Students with disabilities often view writing as a hated task, and as standards move toward embedding writing in more curricular areas, poor writing skills can lead to a broader dislike of school in general. Writing itself is a very personal enterprise, and for a student who struggles with it, writing can be a very personal failure.

When teaching writing, teachers should pay close attention to how students perceive themselves as writers and encourage them to focus on finding and writing in their own unique voice. By modeling the writing process for them—showing how ideas come first, then a rough draft to give them shape, followed by an editing process that addresses the mechanical aspects of the writing—teachers can facilitate student success.

When grading written assignments, teachers should consider grading the first draft for content only, engaging the student in a written dialogue about what he or she is saying in his or her writing. Teachers must quell their urges to point out paragraphing, capitalization, and spelling errors as they read. They should demonstrate the difference between content and mechanics by isolating them in the teaching and evaluation process.

Experienced teachers recognize that writing skill occurs on a developmental continuum, and they help their students to see individual growth along that continuum. Students who understand that what they have to say is unique and valuable are much more open to risking committing their thoughts to paper. They know that the mechanical facets of writing can be addressed concretely farther along in the writing process.

Precautions and Possible Pitfalls

 In recent years, many teachers and parents have lamented the lack of spelling and grammar instruction in schools. Students need to learn the principles behind common spelling patterns as well as the basic grammatical components of standard written English. Most students learn these rules more effectively in context, so teachers should consider embedding a lesson on a specific rule of grammar by asking the students to correct it or apply it in their own writing.

Source

Gregg, N., & Mather, N. (2002). School is fun at recess. *Journal of Learning Disabilities, 35*(1), 7–23.

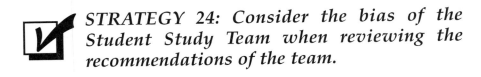

STRATEGY 24: *Consider the bias of the Student Study Team when reviewing the recommendations of the team.*

What the Research Says

In a microethnographic study conducted in two southern elementary schools, multidisciplinary teams were evaluated to identify specific issues that could explain the disproportionate number of African American students who are placed in special education (Knotek, 2003). The study noted that teams of professionals rather than single evaluators are required by law, to avoid the bias in referral that can occur when one person is responsible for the referral process. Interestingly, the study found that bias was more prevalent when students from low-socioeconomic families or students with behavior problems were discussed. If the students discussed had either of these issues, then the discussion became very subjective and the team recommendations became "more reflexive and less reflective" (Knotech, 2003, p. 13).

Application

At most schools, Student Study Teams (child study teams, multidisciplinary teams) consist of a special education teacher, a counselor, a psychologist, an administrator, and a general education teacher. Each of these professionals brings a different perspective to the table as individual student needs are discussed. Participants need to pay close attention to the process and monitor the referrals that comprise the team's history. Trends should be noted. For instance, whether every student of color is being referred to the same program, or every Latino student is being referred for language assessment. Note should also be taken as the team makes suggestions for accommodations for the student in the current placement. Have they considered recommending a change in seat, an afterschool tutoring program, or peer helper prior to suggesting a class change or psychoeducational assessment?

It is also important to keep records of the students discussed and the suggested follow up. Whatever actions the team recommends should be assigned to a specific person to implement and a date should be set for review.

If a trend is noticed, the team should meet outside of its scheduled Student Study Team (SST) meeting to discuss the trend and evaluate whether or not the issue requires further exploration. It is vital that a trained facilitator who is not part of the team help with this discussion, to guard against it becoming a personal attack. Teams gain personalities of their own and can effect change as a group if all members are committed to the process.

Precautions and Possible Pitfalls

Beware of personal bias. Each professional comes to the table with his or her own set of experiences and perspectives as a result of those experiences. It is not uncommon for a new program or a new teacher who is trying a different approach to suddenly become the panacea for all students who are having problems at school. Although this should be rare, be careful to note if the SST is filling a new class or program blindly rather than considering each case individually.

Source

Knotek, S. (2003). Bias in problem solving and the social process of student study teams. *Journal of Special Education, 37*(1), 2–15.

STRATEGY 25: Don't wait for formal testing to begin interventions for students with reading disabilities.

What the Research Says

In a study of 40 first and second graders in Alabama, researchers looked for correlative findings on 20 students who were referred for formal testing and 20 students who were not referred (Sofie & Riccio, 2002). The students were assessed using formal and informal methods. For the formal assessment, researchers administered the WISC-III, the WJ-R (Letter-Word Identification, Passage Comprehension, and Word Attack); CTOPP was used for phonological awareness (Segmenting, Blending, and Elision) and the Dyslexia Screening Instrument was used for the Teacher Rating. For the informal assessment, teachers used curricular-based assessments for fluency. Interestingly, although each of the assessments addressed a different aspect of reading skills, the results were compared and found to be highly correlative.

Given the controversies surrounding norm-referenced testing instruments (cultural bias leading to the disproportionate number of minority and English Language Learner [ELL] students diagnosed with disabilities), curricular-based assessments yielded similar results and inspired teachers to begin interventions immediately. In addition, many of the quick in-class assessments can be used to check the efficacy of the interventions on an ongoing basis.

Application

Many teachers routinely use quick fluency assessments to gauge student placement on the reading continuum. These assessments can be just as effective in determining appropriate reading interventions for students. Some common examples include the use of site word lists and small group read-aloud sessions. By using and acting on the information gained in these informal assessments, teachers can begin to identify and remediate problem areas for students rather than wait for the child to be so far behind that he or she qualifies for special education services.

In higher grades, the gap between fluent readers and reluctant readers widens and continues to represent a greater and greater achievement gap. Student performance on assignments early in the year will often lead teachers to identify which students would benefit from intervention strategies. Suggesting these strategies or inviting students to participate in support programs prior to failing grades or a formal referral process may circumvent the need for alternate placement.

Precautions and Possible Pitfalls

Although most literacy interventions are effective in most cases and certainly will not hinder a student's growth, teachers should not postpone a referral for a student who would benefit from special education services. Instead, they should initiate the referral process according to their site or district policy and then begin intervention strategies that they would normally employ. They should also keep track of what is working, to bring to the team meeting after the student has been formally assessed. One way to accomplish this is by keeping a portfolio of student work samples that highlight student successes as well as areas for growth.

Source

Sofie, C. A., & Riccio, C. A. (2002). A comparison of multiple methods for the identification of children with reading disabilities. *Journal of Learning Disabilities, 35*(3), 234–245.

 STRATEGY 26: Take the time to consider all students when referring students for the Student Study Team or special education assessment, not just the students with obvious behavior issues.

What the Research Says

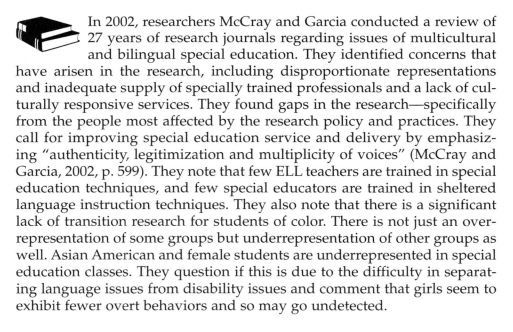 In 2002, researchers McCray and Garcia conducted a review of 27 years of research journals regarding issues of multicultural and bilingual special education. They identified concerns that have arisen in the research, including disproportionate representations and inadequate supply of specially trained professionals and a lack of culturally responsive services. They found gaps in the research—specifically from the people most affected by the research policy and practices. They call for improving special education service and delivery by emphasizing "authenticity, legitimization and multiplicity of voices" (McCray and Garcia, 2002, p. 599). They note that few ELL teachers are trained in special education techniques, and few special educators are trained in sheltered language instruction techniques. They also note that there is a significant lack of transition research for students of color. There is not just an overrepresentation of some groups but underrepresentation of other groups as well. Asian American and female students are underrepresented in special education classes. They question if this is due to the difficulty in separating language issues from disability issues and comment that girls seem to exhibit fewer overt behaviors and so may go undetected.

Application

Although it is common for parents to refer their children for special education testing, the law requires districts to search and identify students with disabilities. Teachers and other staff members need to be cognizant of the issues affecting all students. It is vital that a student who speaks a second language be evaluated in that language for fluency prior to being placed in a classroom for special education service delivery. Likewise, students should not be excluded from receiving services based on language concerns.

Teachers should consider carefully students who quietly fail. It can be a challenge to notice the student who sits in the back of the room barely meeting standards when attention is captured by the boisterous few who are excelling or creating behavior issues. When teachers are grading student papers or entering grades in their grade books, they need to take the time to reflect on each student who is hovering in that D–F range. Considering his or her performance orally in comparison to his or her written assignments may yield some interesting results, as will considering test scores in comparison to project grades. Any discrepancy may be cause for further investigation.

It is always a good idea to ask the student how he or she is doing in other classes or if he or she has noticed that a particular task is difficult. Students know a lot about what is going on with them and can often articulate when a specific learning task is more challenging for them than their peers. Catching that frustration early may facilitate an early intervention.

Precautions and Possible Pitfalls

 Teachers need to be aware of their own biases. All teachers have personal experiences that contribute to their perceptions, and it is important to try to leave them out of the equation when referring students for additional help.

Source

McCray, A. D., & Garcia, S. B. (2002). The stories we must tell: Developing a research agenda for multicultural and bilingual education. *Qualitative Studies in Education, 15*(6), 599–613.

 STRATEGY 27: *Use alternative methods of feedback early in a course to communicate student progress.*

What the Research Says

 Lechner, Brehm, and Zbigniew (1996) investigated four ninth-grade classes concerning the effects of giving grades at an early stage of knowledge acquisition. To show the effects of early marking, four classes were separated into two groups. Both groups received computer-aided instruction and were graded after every step.

The first group did not get to know about their grades, while the second group was informed of their grades. The achievements of the groups were compared on the basis of the grade after every step and on a final test. Students who knew their marks did slightly better on the interim tests. In contrast, on the final test, students who did not know their interim grades did noticeably better according to the research. They were not pushed by pressure of marks. They used additional work to develop self-control. In this way, they dealt with the issue of their learning needs, they understood it profoundly, and they achieved at higher levels.

Giving grades early in the learning process may stimulate students to participate actively in their lessons, but it may undermine achievement in the long run. Previous research provided evidence that students learn because of anxiety over grades or because they get good grades with a minimum of effort. Giving grades early is not beneficial for students who require more time to understand things. They tend to be afraid of saying something wrong and of getting bad grades. Early grading should not be viewed as a judgment of a student's knowledge. It should be viewed more as informative than as judgmental.

Application

 Teachers should avoid giving grades at an early stage of learning. Early marks can easily frustrate students who are not interested in a particular topic or even the whole subject, and their motivation can sink even further. Although for some students early grades can promote rapid success, in some cases this leads to students resting on their laurels. During the period students are acquiring new knowledge, the teacher should use grades sparingly and utilize other forms of feedback.

Teachers need to remember that not all feedback needs to be evaluated with a grade. The process of learning and putting together a product is increasingly seen as more important than the finished product itself. Simply checking off a step or stamping work as completed before moving on to the next could be enough incentive (with feedback) to keep instruction (and learning) moving.

Alternative forms of feedback could include written teacher comments, rubrics, oral commentary, and peer evaluation. The more specific and constructive feedback a student receives, the more he or she will understand what step to take next.

Precautions and Possible Pitfalls

Teachers should not stop all assessment during the early stage of learning. First, students need assessment to evaluate or at least estimate their own achievement. Several smaller quizzes can also reduce the anxiety that can accompany one larger exam. In addition, teachers will always find some students who are entirely motivated by grades. Therefore, during the early learning phase, teachers should use oral or nonverbal assessment techniques.

Source

Lechner, H. J., Brehm, R. I., & Zbigniew, M. (1996). Zensierung und ihr einfluß auf die leistung der schüler [Influence of marks on student achievement]. *Pädagogik und Schulalltag, 51*(3), 371–379.

 STRATEGY 28: Consider alternate assessment styles and instruments when teaching students with learning issues.

What the Research Says

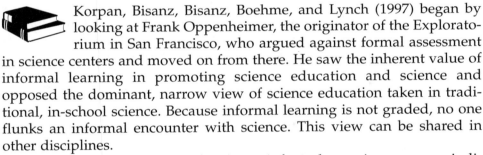

Korpan, Bisanz, Bisanz, Boehme, and Lynch (1997) began by looking at Frank Oppenheimer, the originator of the Exploratorium in San Francisco, who argued against formal assessment in science centers and moved on from there. He saw the inherent value of informal learning in promoting science education and science and opposed the dominant, narrow view of science education taken in traditional, in-school science. Because informal learning is not graded, no one flunks an informal encounter with science. This view can be shared in other disciplines.

Some researchers believe that many informal experiences are so individual and multifaceted that they cannot be assessed with letter grades or scores. Some see the lack of evaluation as an obvious strength in engaging individuals in a more social, open-ended, learner-directed experience, with a less planned and nonevaluative contact with science. Trying to evaluate so many potential unintended outcomes is just not fair to students. Out of four research papers that examined out-of-school informal educational activities, all used students' written reflections (some used a rubric to guide students' responses) to survey the students' perception of how much they learned and its quality.

Application

The assessment instruments identified in this research were not designed to yield a score or grade. They were designed to measure the overall effectiveness of the encounter. This information could then be used to modify the encounter itself and not rate the students' success or failure. Movies, plays, art galleries, and a host of other out-of-classroom activities can be used as authentic curricula to provide interesting and motivating learning pathways.

One study featured assessment that was produced by parents interacting with their child. Students were stimulated by their parents' involvement and the students felt comfortable with their parents. Researchers found this type of assessment to suffer from low reliability and validity, but it had its advantages. The collaborative, nonthreatening nature of the informal project fostered active and meaningful learning and an integrated school, home, and community. These kinds of activities can be particularly helpful for providing information to the IEP team.

It's clear that traditional content assessment may miss the point of the out-of-school experience or informal in-school learning. There is a wider range of attributes and facets that need to be measured, and a content test would send the wrong message to students about what is important. Extending the experience by expanding it with a related performance-based project, writing activity, or other application would be a better gauge of mastery than a traditional test. Ramsey-Gassert (1997) felt that projects with appropriate scoring rubrics, where students combine discipline content from the classroom and the informal experience, are the best way for students to demonstrate this type of learning. Ultimately the teacher wants to facilitate enthusiasm and motivation. It is often a positive educational experience for students to create their own rubrics identifying key concepts in a particular subject area.

Precautions and Possible Pitfalls

Consider a student with special needs who performs poorly in the traditional classroom yet exhibits enthusiasm and interest in more hands-on activities and participation in out-of-school learning experiences. This situation presents teachers with a dilemma as to how to encourage students and not penalize them with narrow-range, traditional classroom assessment devices. The teacher should not turn off the students' enthusiasm. Balancing opportunities for successful assessment and evaluation gives students in this group more than one pathway to find and demonstrate success. Oral presentations, project display boards, student videos, computer-generated presentations (e.g., PowerPoint), and other instructional outcomes can help these students find success.

Another problem is providing equal access and opportunity for all students in class. Sometimes parental support is not available to all students. The teacher needs to make learning outside the classroom an option with an in-school component for those who can't participate in off-campus activities. For example, students who are unable to attend a local production of *Death of a Salesman* could check the video out of the school library or watch it in the classroom during lunch.

Sources

Korpan, C. A., Bisanz, G. L., Bisanz, J., Boehme, C., & Lynch, M. A. (1997). What did you learn outside of school today? Using structured interviews to document home and community activities related to science and technology. *Science Education, 81*(6), 651–662.

Kurth, L. A., & Richmond, G. (1999). Moving from outside to inside: High school students' use of apprenticeship as a vehicle for entering the culture and practice of science. *Journal of Research in Science Teaching, 36*(6), 677–697.

Ramsey-Gassert, L. (1997). Learning science beyond the classroom. *Elementary School Journal, 97*(4), 95–113.

STRATEGY 29: *Positive feedback heightens students' confidence.*

What the Research Says

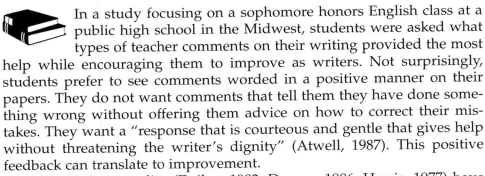

In a study focusing on a sophomore honors English class at a public high school in the Midwest, students were asked what types of teacher comments on their writing provided the most help while encouraging them to improve as writers. Not surprisingly, students prefer to see comments worded in a positive manner on their papers. They do not want comments that tell them they have done something wrong without offering them advice on how to correct their mistakes. They want a "response that is courteous and gentle that gives help without threatening the writer's dignity" (Atwell, 1987). This positive feedback can translate to improvement.

At least three studies (Daiker, 1983; Dragga, 1986; Harris, 1977) have shown that teachers usually do not praise students' writing often enough. Daiker, Kerek, and Morenberg (1986) found that the vast majority of comments (89.4%) "cited error or found fault; on . . . 10.6% of them were comments of praise" (p. 104).

Application

The goal of student writing is improvement; therefore, the more specific a teacher can be with comments on students' work, with thorough explanations and deserved praise for what they have done well (as opposed to taking the dreaded red pen and marking only what is wrong), the more likely students will feel supported and will work to improve. Teachers must also look at their own commenting style. Are comments only on form or is content included? Are the ideas the student is proposing considered? If the objective is to improve over several drafts, then certainly grammatical errors such as spelling and punctuation should not comprise the majority of a teacher's comments. These parts of writing are important, but can be revised in a later draft, after the student has the content problems ironed out. Do students know what is right with their work as well as what needs to be done to correct mistakes? Telling a student to be more specific has little or no meaning for them if they do not know which part of their text needs to be more specific.

Teachers can model effective correction techniques by using a generic or teacher-created writing sample that the class corrects as a group. By combining this approach with a rubric, students can make the connection between what is required and what a specific writing sample demonstrates.

Precautions and Possible Pitfalls

Whether they are writing papers for English, science, or history, most students want their writing to reflect improvement. Teachers need to be careful not to use praise that is too general or of a patronizing nature. At the beginning of a course, teachers should go over their specific commenting style with students and whether they will use symbols as well as written comments. Teachers should make sure students understand what these symbols mean. In addition to written comments, teachers should talk to students about their papers on a regular basis and encourage students to ask questions if the comments they are given aren't clear.

Sources

Atwell, N. (1987). *"In the middle": Writing, reading, and learning with adolescents.* Portsmouth, NH: Boynton/Cook.

Bardine, B. A. (1999). Students' perceptions of written teacher comments: What do they say about how we respond to them? *High School Journal, 82*(4), 248–249.

Daiker, D. (1983, March). *The teacher's options in responding to student writing.* Paper presented at the annual conference on College Composition and Communication, Washington, DC.

Daiker, D. A., Kerek, A., & Morenberg, M. (1986). *The writer's options: Combining composing* (3rd ed.). New York: Harper.

Dragga, S. (1986, March). *Praiseworthy grading: A teacher's alternative to editing error.* Paper presented at the Conference on College Composition and Communication, New Orleans.

Harris, W. H. (1977). Teacher response to student writing: A study of the response pattern of high school teachers to determine the basis for teacher judgment of student writing. *Research in the Teaching of English, 11,* 175–185.

STRATEGY 30: When evaluating student performance, consider the data collection methods used and the natural decline of ability due to late transitions.

What the Research Says

Ysseldyke and Bielinski (2002) examined the alarming decline of special education students' performance compared with their age-appropriate general education peers over a period of five years in Texas. They found that testing statistics regarding 217,519 students were developed by averaging the test scores of the two groups of students and then charting them, noting the divergent gap that emerged. They discovered that many administrative decisions were based on this data regarding the efficacy of special education programs. Upon closer examination of the statistical methodology, the researchers found that the data was compiled using a cohort-dynamic method, meaning that students in each group were compared to the other group year after year. The groups included students who had transitioned in and out of the special education program. Using a cohort-static method, however, yielded a very different set of results. By assessing the test results of the students who were in special education or general education at the beginning and then tracking their progress over the five years, the disparate gap was not as significant. The cohort-dynamic method failed to account for higher achieving students in special education who were transitioned to general education and the lowest achieving general education students who were transitioned to special education producing the lowest achievers in the special education group over time.

Application

Before assessing the efficacy of a special education program, accurate data collection methods must be used. As students progress and transition out of special education, attention should be paid to that success. Likewise, students who are tested and transitioned into special education in upper grades should not be factored into the overall performance of the special education program but should be considered by themselves. Federal law calls for individual consideration of students with disabilities specifically because their needs are so individual. Special education programs logically require the same kind of individual consideration.

Precautions and Possible Pitfalls

 In these times of high stakes testing and public accountability for all students, greater attention must be paid to the data that is being collected. Teachers may find it useful to access previous standardized test results for their students to help guide their instructional plans. In addition, teachers may want to collect their own data on students' progress and performance to bring to the discussion table when program changes are needed.

Source

Ysseldyke, J., & Bielinski, J. (2002). Effect of different methods of reporting and reclassification on trends in test scores for students with disabilities. *Exceptional Children, 68*(2),189–201.

 STRATEGY 31: Consider alternative grading systems as an adaptable accommodation for diverse student populations in general education classrooms.

What the Research Says

Hendrickson, Gable, and Manning (1999) begin by characterizing today's classrooms and assessment and evaluation dilemmas regarding grading of diverse populations. They follow this with examinations of alternative grading systems and functions of student grades. They propose grading options and discuss the strengths and weaknesses of each. They offer a large range of options and discussion of the pros and cons of grading strategies. The research points dissect many assessment options that could be used or modified to meet the needs to individual teachers, schools, and communities.

Hendrickson et al. (1999) examined campuses with multiple and unified grading systems. They found schools tended to explore and establish multiple grading systems, but the authors' experience suggests that multiple systems (one for challenged students and one for mainstream students) only add to confusion for all stakeholders. There is a growing awareness that alternative grading practices are appropriate for students with special needs only to the extent that the system doesn't discriminate. This means that the grading system for students with special learning needs should be available to other students as well. For example, if an asterisk (*) is used to indicate an alternative grading system on the report card of a student with a disability, then the asterisk should be used for any other student for whom a different standard is applied. In this way the special education student is not singled out.

What Grading Options Can Be Considered?

1. IEP-Based Grading

Grades are based on goals and objectives articulated in the IEP. The student's strengths and weaknesses are taken into consideration and testing accommodations and grading criteria are specifically described. The accommodations and criteria are based on input from members of the IEP team.

2. Individual Contracts

Grades are awarded in accordance with a written agreement between the student and the teacher. The learning activities, quantity and quality of work, and time allotted to earn a specific grade are specified. A contract can be an extension of criterion-referenced, IEP-based grading.

3. Multiple Grades

Several separate grades are earned. For instance, the student may receive a grade for competence or mastery of content, demonstrated effort, and progress toward a final objective. A single grade may be calculated based on ability, effort, and growth of the student. This grade may be norm-referenced (i.e., judged against a specific standard).

4. Shared Grades

Grades are collaboratively determined between the general and special education teachers, based on preestablished percent, criterion, or normative standards. Grades earned by the student in the resource classroom and the general education classroom can be averaged.

5. Checklist Evaluations

Specific skills and knowledge is described in narrative statements, often presented sequentially or in a task analysis format. After each statement there are columns (or a Likert-type scale) where the skills and knowledge can be checked off (rated) as being completed/mastered, in further work, or yet to be attempted, according to a specific performance criteria.

6. Portfolio Systems

Work samples representing various stages of skill development (e.g., writing assignment), curriculum-based evaluation data and products, self-evaluation statements, or multiple scores can be evaluated against either a percent or criterion-referenced standard.

7. Narrative Reports

Written statements kept chronologically or on an evaluation form with various headings generally are employed by teachers to report a student's effort, progress and growth, and level of achievement. Students can be evaluated on a percent, criterion-referenced, or norm-referenced basis.

8. Parent/Family Conferences

Regularly scheduled meetings with parents or family and the teachers and students can be used to review student progress, discuss educational issues, examine student work products and performance, and discuss strengths and weaknesses. Conferences can be used to supplement other forms of student grading.

9. Point Systems

The student may earn a grade or grades based on total points earned for completing various assignments and assuming various responsibilities. For example, homework assignments completed may be worth 10 points, weekly quizzes worth 20 points, and so on. A student's total number of points for the day, week, or other period of time are converted to letter or numerical grades. Pass-fail can also be used. The student is expected to complete minimum levels of competency for a given course to pass. The pass requirement can be connected to a percent or criterion levels of attendance, work completed, accuracy of work, and participation in class, or reflect a normative perspective.

10. Weighted Grading

Student performance, effort, participation, and other variables are graded independently and weighted differently in arriving at the final grade.

11. Self-Comparison Grades

The student is evaluated based on the relative amount of gain from one point in time to another. Learning and performance trend lines can be used to determine whether the student is achieving within, below, or above an acceptable level or range.

Application

Today's very diverse classrooms can present some serious soul searching and challenges regarding assessment and grading. The greatest challenge is to find a way to meet the needs of a wide range of student development levels, abilities, and interests. Teachers are routinely faced with modifying curriculum or instruction to accommodate individual student needs and are constantly pulled between two masters. One is the force of "excellence in education" through more rigorous standards and increasing accountability for student mastery of academics. The other is to integrate students with special challenges into the general mainstream population. Often this brings together two conflicting expectations into regular classroom practice and curricular strategies. This is especially true with student assessment and grading. Most teachers understand making accommodations for students with disabilities; many often forget that alternative grading systems should also be considered and included as an accommodation.

With the growing diversity of school populations, traditional policies regarding grading are coming under growing debate. Grades and grading are very personal issues for both individual educators and their students. Does the same grade mean the same thing in the class next door or for the student in the next seat? Grades represent a communication of judgment regarding the extent to which students grasp subject matter and document overall class performance. For most, grades are an effective tool for motivating students, reinforcing the value of learning, and evaluating and communicating the outcome(s) of instruction. The growing diversity of today's classroom requires educators to reexamine stereotypical assessment, evaluation, and grading techniques. There is a risk that current practices can short-change significant numbers of students in a conflicting mix of philosophies. The goal here is to be realistic, flexible, and nondiscriminatory. In today's schools, the general educator will be asked to become a more active member of the teams serving students with learning or other disabilities. Teachers need to be able to establish grading policies and utilize practices that fit the needs of a changing student population and students with disabilities in regular classrooms. Hopefully the ideas presented above will open the discussion and offer creative options for specific sites as they consider what grading options are available.

Precautions and Potential Pitfalls

A university admissions official on a campus of the State University of New York was commenting on the differences between transcripts from schools on the south and north shore of Long Island, New York. He explained that grades from schools on the south shore seemed to be inflated, with "A" students scoring lower on the SAT test than "A" students on the north shore. He felt that the SAT normalized differences in grading philosophies and that grades by themselves can't be trusted. The debate about what grades should mean will always go on. Each school features a political climate that produces subtle and not-so-subtle forces that will affect how students are assessed and evaluated. Diverse classrooms provide some of the greatest challenges and grades are one of the biggest. There is no one right answer.

Source

Hendrickson, J. M., Gable, R. A., & Manning, M. L. (1999). Can everyone make the grade? Some thoughts on student grading and contemporary classrooms. *High School Journal, 82*(4), 248.

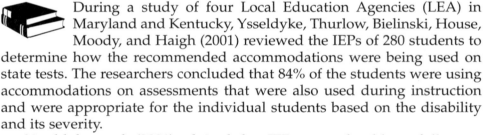

STRATEGY 32: Ensure that the accommodations a student needs to benefit from instruction are the same accommodations that are used during assessment.

What the Research Says

During a study of four Local Education Agencies (LEA) in Maryland and Kentucky, Ysseldyke, Thurlow, Bielinski, House, Moody, and Haigh (2001) reviewed the IEPs of 280 students to determine how the recommended accommodations were being used on state tests. The researchers concluded that 84% of the students were using accommodations on assessments that were also used during instruction and were appropriate for the individual students based on the disability and its severity.

Ysseldyke et al. (2001) advised that IEP teams should carefully consider the individual student's needs prior to recommending accommodations for instruction and assessment. The most common accommodations were reading aloud to students with reading difficulties, taking dictation for students with writing difficulties, calculators for students with math difficulties, and extra time or breaks. The researchers found that a minimum of one month of using the specific accommodation was advisable before the student used the accommodation during the assessment.

Application

Sometimes, in an effort to help students who have disabilities, IEP teams will recommend every accommodation that comes to mind. Kindly, they reason, "Wouldn't every student benefit from extra time so he or she doesn't feel pressured? Preferential seating because it's near the teacher? Material read aloud because he or she will receive extra attention?" and so on. Although these things look good on paper, receiving an accommodation can be embarrassing for a student, particularly if it is one that the student doesn't really need or benefit from.

Based on the collected data, the IEP team suggests appropriate accommodations, but it is up to the student and the teacher, working together and keeping the lines of communication open, to ensure that the accommodation is really serving the needs of the student. Teachers need to offer the specific accommodation to the student as the IEP requires, but they need to take it one step further by noting whether the student benefited. An easy way to do this is simply to note on the top of any given assignment or assessment what accommodations were offered, used, and the outcome. For example, if the student needed a calculator to complete the class work, the teacher can note "Calc used" along with the score. This data will help the student and the IEP team to determine which accommodations the student really benefits from.

Precautions and Possible Pitfalls

Teachers need to take care not to make the mistake of not offering a student an accommodation that is specified in the IEP because they feel the student doesn't need it. Failure to comply with the IEP, a legal document, may result in a lawsuit. The student may choose not to use the accommodation, and that is up to him or her. Teachers should make a note of what was offered and whether the student refused. The only way to change the accommodations noted in an IEP is to request a meeting to amend it.

Source

Ysseldyke, J., Thurlow, M., Bielinski, J., House, A., Moody, M., & Haigh, J. (2001). The relationship between instructional and assessment accommodations in an inclusive state accountability system. *Journal of Learning Disabilities, 34*(3), 212–221.

STRATEGY 33: Use portfolios to collect evidence of student performance that allows teachers to compare, contrast, and counteract narrowly defined test scores, which may or may not accurately reflect a diverse learner's ability.

What the Research Says

Reflections over a 10-year period explored the many teaching and learning experiences involving portfolio assessment. Timely and careful assessment and evaluation painted a clear picture of what portfolios are and what portfolios aren't. Influenced by Howard Gardner's multiple intelligences, the faculty of Crow Island School in Winnetke, Illinois, assessed and evaluated their 10-year journey and the evolution of their portfolio thinking. Overall, they found portfolios fulfilled the promises they felt portfolios held when they began. The staff defined and refined the roles of all stakeholders in the portfolio concept and today continue to gain a more in-depth view of their students as learners through the use of the their full site-based, student-centered portfolio vision (Hebert, 1998).

Application

Points to consider when thinking about portfolios:

1. Portfolios in education, by most definitions, are created to tell a story. Don't be too rigid when deciding what goes into one. Consider allowing and helping the students to decide what goes into the "story" of their learning and growth. Are the portfolios going to be teacher-centered or student-centered? Who decides what goes into one?

2. Decide what work will go home and what should stay in the portfolio.

3. Whose portfolio is it? Should the teacher assume the role of a portfolio manager and let students decide what will counterbalance test scores and enter the portfolio? When students are first discovering what a portfolio is, they require a scaffolding strategy.

4. Grading or attaching a letter grade to a portfolio seems to run contrary to the nature of the concept. Give it some thought.

5. Select a time frame for the history of the learning a portfolio might represent. Is a portfolio a year's worth of work?

6. For some students, "telling" a long-term story is too abstract. Defining an audience for the work contributes to a more concrete picture.

7. Attach meaning to each piece in a portfolio by asking students to write a short reason for its inclusion into the story. "Reflection tag" was the term used in the research literature. This contributes to the

student's metacognitive growth and attaches further value and meaning to the individual content.

8. Deliberately teach parents about the value of student portfolios: what they mean, how they reflect the curriculum and the students. Portfolios can also be a powerful tool in IEP goal development.

Precautions and Possible Pitfalls

On the surface, portfolios sound like a simple concept. Do not underestimate the learning curve for teachers, students, and parents if the concept is to really function at its best. Expect some frustration during the implementation and transition to portfolio adoption.

Source

Hebert, E. (1998). Lessons learned about student portfolios. *Phi Delta Kappan,* 79(8), 583–585.

 STRATEGY 34: *Consider using a variety of assessments that accurately reflect the course objectives and standards.*

What the Research Says

In an analysis of 309 lessons designed by 65 preservice teachers, Campbell and Evans (2000) discovered that few teachers implemented the concepts they had studied in their educational measurement coursework. This lack of conceptual implementation made it difficult for the researchers to link the curricular goals to the instruction and ultimately student mastery. The researchers also noted that more than 23% of the lesson plans had either omitted or contained nonobservable instructional objectives. Although 113 plans included rubrics for assessments, only 8 were complete. Consistent scoring methods were also a significant concern.

It seems that although the teachers agreed that assessment was an important aspect of instruction (81%), they seemed to view instruction and assessment as separate facets of a lesson rather than parts of the same process to inform future instruction. The researchers noted that the technical aspects of test construction were demonstrated but remarked that the inferences made about student progress were weak.

Application

 During the history of public education, there has never been a better time in which to find help on assessment and instructional practices. Today course content has never been more analyzed by state framework writers, educational agencies, special interest groups, and parent organizations. The best of them feature not only content outlines but pedagogical and assessment suggestions and guidelines. In addition, most textbook publishers (who design their books based on the same documents) provide instruction and assessment strategies connected to their book's content. Many also provide alternative assessment suggestions for teachers working with students who require modifications, accommodations, or enrichment.

Most subject content frameworks are now accessible via the Internet, and most textbooks come with ample support material. In addition, many teachers utilize assessment strategies that connect to skills required on those standardized tests students are taking. Teachers should analyze and utilize them all within their personal instructional context. Assessment should be the research that drives further instruction, not simply a summary of student mastery.

It's clear the resources are there. The dilemma for most teachers is deciding which to use. Some of these resources offer more valid and reliable information. The key is finding a secure bridge between instructional goals, classroom instruction, and assessment. Also, all teachers come with their own ideas about assessment, and many also incorporate their district's goals. Some framework and supplemental textbook information seems written by people who have never been in a classroom. Some others stand out and seem to have been written with just the district's goals in mind. Teachers should survey as much information as they can access before synthesizing their own strategies.

The strategy for most teachers is to construct the unit or lesson in a complete package with equal attention to goals and objectives; instructional delivery systems; and fair, reliable, and valid assessment strategies. If assessment is considered and addressed before beginning instruction, teachers will find peace of mind and security as they move the students toward final assessment. They'll know what their students need to be successful as they go, and they always have that in the back of their minds. In this way, they can always make adjustments to instruction, shorten or lengthen the pace, or simplify or rework instructional trouble spots or tweak the assessment a bit if necessary, particularly for those students who require additional supports. There is truth in the saying, "If you don't know where you are going, you will probably never get there."

Precautions and Possible Pitfalls

For many teachers, politics plays a heavy role in assessment. Teachers often find themselves split between using assessment instruments and strategies that prepare students for standardized testing formats and using more authentic assessments. A solution to this dilemma is to develop a variety of assessment options for students. Many teachers find that providing choice for their students contributes to student buy-in as well as making for more stimulating and less repetitive grading for the teacher.

Source

Campbell, C., & Evans J. A.(2000). Investigation of preservice teachers' classroom assessment practices during student teaching. *Journal of Educational Research, 93*(6), 350–356.

 STRATEGY 35: Make sure either the expert who conducted the student's assessment or another person who is trained to interpret the findings is present at the IEP meeting.

What the Research Says

In an analysis of 45 published due-process hearings, Yell and Dragow (2000) determined that the majority of district losses were due to errors in the IEP process. The IEP is the legal documentation of a student's FAPE (free and appropriate public education), and its development is carefully guided by federal law. The problems identified included:

- An absence of an expert in the area of autism at the development of a student with autism's IEP
- Samples of 103 assessments where only 8 assessment strategies were deemed complete
- The absence of the concepts of reliability and validity
- Twenty-three percent that featured nonobservable objectives although the majority recognized the need

Application

With today's busy schedules, coupled with the budget cuts that many districts are facing, it can be a challenge to gather together the various professionals to meet together as an assessment team. Psychologists are often split between sites, and speech pathologists may only work part time. There is no question that having all the professionals together to present the assessment findings is valuable, but it is also required by law. The law recognizes that it is essential that a student's assessment results are correctly interpreted by the professional who conducted the assessment(s), whenever possible. Parents and students may have questions regarding the validity as well as the implications of certain results, and those questions need to be answered before placement can be determined. In addition, other team members may have noted similar trends in their own assessment findings, and the collaborative effort of the team will yield the best result.

In cases where the psychologist or speech therapist simply cannot attend, another professional who is specifically trained in that area may present and interpret the assessment results for the team. In these cases, it can be advisable for the professional who conducted the assessment to call the parent and explain the results over the phone as well as answer any additional questions. This practice does not preclude the need for a trained professional at the meeting.

Precautions and Possible Pitfalls

The team member who is chairing the meeting and taking the required notes for the IEP meeting should include a notation that assessment results were presented by a trained professional. In addition, if questions arise that cannot be addressed without the professional who administered the test, then the meeting should be adjourned and rescheduled.

Source

Yell, M. L., & Drasgow, E. (2000). Litigating a free appropriate public education: The Lovass hearings and cases. *Journal of Special Education, 33*(4), 205–215.

4

Classroom Management and Discipline

So many things are possible just as long as you don't know they're impossible.

—Norton Juster

☑ *STRATEGY 36: Consider implementing a self-regulation model of behavior management when teaching a student diagnosed with ADHD.*

What the Research Says

 A 1996 study of 52 third- and fourth-grade students from 17 schools in Valencia, Spain, examined the effects of a multicomponent approach to teaching students identified with ADHD (Miranda, 2001). The students were pretested using psychoeducational instruments, behavior rating scales, and classroom observations. Focusing on activity, impulse control, and attention, the researchers trained the teachers in specific intervention strategies. Students were then trained to use self-instruction and reinforced self-evaluation techniques to help them manage their own behavior. Using the "Think Aloud" procedure developed by Camp and Bush (1981), the students began to adapt their classroom behaviors.

The experimental group was given additional instruction in three phases. The first phase was an active discussion focusing on classroom rules of conduct. The second phase was the discussion and establishment of a four-point, self-scoring system corresponding to the behavioral rules. The third phase involved a discussion to determine the prizes and their corresponding point values.

The study determined that after four months, the students in the experimental group had made significant growth in comparison to the control group. Hyperactive and impulsive behaviors were reduced and self-control was increased. Teachers also noted an increase in academic performance in math and the natural sciences (Miranda, 2001).

Application

 Although many students are routinely medicated to address the concerns of ADHD, without positive instruction in self-control, medication may not be sufficient to ensure that a student has the opportunity to learn and the teacher has the opportunity to teach. By developing a plan with a student to address the specific behaviors that are interfering with the learning process, the teacher can facilitate the intervention process.

Begin with a clear identification of the classroom rules and then assign a point value to each rule so the student can begin to prioritize the behaviors in a positive context. Although tangible rewards are effective for younger students, for older students, a variety of options are available, including student-choice assignments, extra credit, retake privileges, and so on. The student can use a chart or card to track his or her points as the positive observation of the rules occur. This is contrary to a negative, infraction-based approach that must be managed by the teacher. At the end of the designated period, the teacher and student meet for a positive discussion of the points earned and the prize can be exchanged.

Precautions and Possible Pitfalls

Teachers should be careful when assigning "rewards" so they don't inadvertently devalue their own curriculum. Excusing a student from writing an essay sends the message that writing is unpleasant and to be avoided. Likewise, missing homework sends the message that homework doesn't really contribute to learning and can be excused without consequence.

Sources

Camp, B. W., & Bush, M. A. (1981). *Think aloud: Increasing social and cognitive skills. A problem-solving program for children (primary level).* Champaign, IL: Research Press.

Miranda, A. (2001). Effectiveness of a school-based multicomponent program for the treatment of children with ADHD. *Journal of Learning Disabilities, 35*(6), 546–563.

STRATEGY 37: Actively address negative behaviors in the classroom by considering all aspects of the environment created for students.

What the Research Says

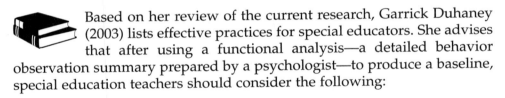

Based on her review of the current research, Garrick Duhaney (2003) lists effective practices for special educators. She advises that after using a functional analysis—a detailed behavior observation summary prepared by a psychologist—to produce a baseline, special education teachers should consider the following:

1. Gradually introducing new routines and stimuli

2. Focusing on transitions to prevent behaviors by warning students, using proximity control, redirecting inappropriate behaviors, and dismissing students in small groups rather than the whole group

3. Evaluating the level of noise in a classroom, as many students are sensitive to noise and are distracted by the loudest ambient noise

4. Addressing the personal connection by creating positive relationships (acknowledging birthdays, illness, knowing student names, etc.)

5. Teaching interventions for behaviors including self-talk (moving from aloud to silent)

6. Providing opportunities for physical movement

7. Teaching the rules and avoiding no-win arguments

8. Using token economies, contingency contracts, and cognitive behavioral therapy to teach more functional behaviors

9. Using peer support, family involvement, and social skills interventions

She also recommended that teachers and parents visit the interactive Web site www.behavioradvisor.com.

Application

 Years ago, experts advised new parents to get on their hands and knees to evaluate their home for potential hazards during their childproofing efforts. The same analogy can be applied to the classroom. By viewing their classrooms through the eyes of their students, particularly those with behavioral issues, teachers will gain valuable insights into the best way to prevent negative behaviors.

Teachers should begin by evaluating the physical environment. They should consider the effects that the desk arrangement may have on the students who need to move around frequently. Considering noise, temperature, and how the layout is used when teaching are important. Teachers should note problem areas and either change them or teach students how to react appropriately to the situation.

Next, teachers should evaluate their classroom procedures. It is always worth the time to teach the classroom procedures rather than allowing students to discover the rules over time. Teachers should examine how they facilitate transitions for their students. By minimizing abrupt changes and preparing students ahead of time for a specific activity, teachers will increase students' ability to behave appropriately.

Then teachers should consider their curriculum and its impact on their specific students. Are there areas that seem to frustrate the students? If so, teachers should prepare them for the frustration by letting them know that the material is challenging and reassuring them that it will be covered in several ways to help their understanding. Teachers should consider adding high-interest pieces to capture students' attention and bring relevance to their instruction.

Lastly, teachers must consider the individual student. Having open communication with the student, parent, and other service providers will facilitate the student's efforts in improving behavior. As noted in the research, teachers may want to consult www.behavioradvisor.com regarding specific student behaviors. The site offers some excellent information about behavior modification techniques in addition to a bulletin board that allows teachers to post specific questions, which will be answered by a variety of teachers who frequent the Web site.

Precautions and Possible Pitfalls

It is important to remember to give the changes made in the environment, routine, or instruction time before evaluating their efficacy. After making a significant adjustment in the usual practice, it is normal to see a honeymoon period followed by an increase in negative behaviors prior to seeing the negative behavior diminish. Teachers need to know that this part of the process and refrain from making too many changes at once. By keeping accurate logs of observable behaviors, teachers can more accurately determine which environmental factors are affecting students.

Source

Garrick Duhaney, L. M. (2003). A practical approach to managing the behaviors of students with ADD. *Intervention in School & Clinic, 38*(52), 267–280.

STRATEGY 38: Consider using a reflective narrative model to facilitate behavior modification decisions.

What the Research Says

In an effort to move teachers from a reactive behavior modification approach to a proactive model, graduate students at the College of New Jersey used an adapted narrative model to focus on behavior change for students with problem behaviors. The narrative model used is broken into two parts. The first half is devoted to the observation of the behavior, including items like antecedents, behavior, and consequences. The second half is devoted to reflections on the part of the teacher. Teachers were encouraged to write down their thoughts regarding the behavior and the efficacy of any intervention attempted (Rao, Hoyer, Meehan, Young, & Guerrera, 2003).

One advantage of the narrative log was the empathy it elicited from the teacher observers. By viewing the behavior as a means for a student rather than just trying to extinguish it, the teachers felt a greater sense of understanding. Likewise, the narrative lent itself to placing the behaviors in the context of the curriculum. Teachers were able to focus on the skills required for the specific academic task and draw conclusions from that angle. Environmental issues that may be contributing to difficult behaviors are easily noted in the narrative format. The reflective format encourages teachers to develop and focus on the behaviors that need to be addressed and also allows for some brainstorming that may lead to multiple approaches rather than a reactive constant. Finally, the reflective aspects of the narrative approach allow teachers to examine their own feelings about the specific behaviors.

Application

Many teachers are familiar with the California Formative Assessment and Support System for Teachers (CFASST) "Plan, Teach, Reflect, Apply" approach to curriculum design, yet few teachers take advantage of the value of reflection when it comes to behavior management. Although it is fairly common to see teachers documenting student behaviors and their antecedents and consequences, it is less common to have teachers personally reflect on their observations. Reflection can be written narrative or oral dialogue, but in order to be effective, it must include attitude and feelings about the context and the behavior from both the student's and the teacher's perspectives. Students choose behaviors because they meet a need. By identifying the need, a teacher may be able to move a student into a more desirable behavior that meets the same need.

Precautions and Possible Pitfalls

Even though a teacher may reflect honestly negative feelings in his or her narratives, it is important to remember that any written documents can be subpoenaed in a court of law. It is essential that the narrative concern the behavior, not the student, and be written in professional terms.

Source

Rao, S., Hoyer, L., Meehan, K., Young, L., & Guerrera, A. (2003). Using narrative logs: Understanding students' challenging behaviors. *Teaching Exceptional Children, 35*(5), 22–30.

 STRATEGY 39: *Consider increasing the pace of instruction rather than reducing the pace when teaching students with special needs.*

What the Research Says

 In his review of current practice and the research behind it, Heward (2003) cautions teachers who accept the idea that special educators should be patient and lower their expectations for their students and ultimately slow the pace of instruction in an effort to demonstrate that patience. Heward argues that slowing the pace of instruction not only contributes to students' lagging attention but misbehavior and lack of skill acquisition as well. Heward cites the study of Ernsbarger (2002), in which students who were prompted using a variety of visual, auditory, and tactile prompts made greater reading skill gains than those who were required to respond independently. Wait time was decreased as reading skills increased, until students were able to respond quickly and independently.

Application

 Although there are many times when a good teacher will allow a student the needed "wait time" in order to facilitate a response, waiting may not always be the most effective practice. In applications requiring rapid responses from students with special needs, teachers should scaffold student responses by offering either visual or oral cues to facilitate skill acquisition. Learning math facts and sight words are two examples of curriculum that may be enhanced with a series of quick prompts. These cues can be faded over time as the response becomes more automatic for the student. Teachers should pay close attention to student progress and level of interest, and use rapid pacing to heighten student interest and encourage the volume of responses.

Precautions and Possible Pitfalls

Teachers should be careful to monitor the pacing to keep students' attention focused. They should not increase the pace to the point that students become frustrated or slow the pace to the point that the students become distracted. It is important that teachers remember the variety of academic skill levels every group of students presents and keep those abilities in mind when planning and delivering instruction.

Sources

Ernsbarger, S. C. (2002). Simple, affordable and effective strategies for prompting reading behavior. *Reading and Writing Quarterly,18*(3), 279–285.

Heward, W. L. (2003). Ten faulty notions about teaching and learning that hinder the effectiveness of special education. *Journal of Special Education, 36*(4), 186–206.

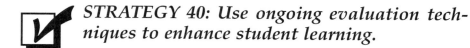

STRATEGY 40: *Use ongoing evaluation techniques to enhance student learning.*

What the Research Says

In a study of 12 elementary school teachers who were identified as "good" teachers by their peers, Alexandrin (2003) documented the ongoing evaluation practices of 10 of these teachers who used continuous evaluative techniques to inform their practice working with special education students and diverse learners. Alexandrin noted that teachers who use ongoing evaluation in inclusive classrooms have a better idea of which students have mastered a concept, grasped a new pattern, or who need the material presented in a different format. The results of the focus group study yielded six main ideas:

1. Move around the classroom.

2. Observe student work frequently.

3. Have discussions with students.

4. View behaviors as indicators of understanding.

5. Don't view teachers as the sole problem solvers.

6. Have high expectations of all students.

Application

Teachers should consider using a "scan and plan" approach after delivering direct instruction and when students are independently working. They can make a quick "scan" of student progress by walking around the classroom and noting how students are working. If they notice that the same question comes up several times, or students seem to be slowing at the same spot, they can adjust their "plan" and quickly reteach that piece. Teachers should check for understanding with application questions that allow students to apply their learning. Teachers should ask "What if" questions to help students own their new knowledge by defining it more concretely. Encouraging students to help each other as they develop understanding of new concepts will facilitate student learning.

Precautions and Possible Pitfalls

 Although some teachers like to use a tally sheet or narrative form to assess student progress as they circulate, avoid any labor-intensive system that takes more time than it saves in the long run.

Source

Alexandrin, J. R. (2003). Using continuous, constructive classroom evaluations. *Teaching Exceptional Children, 36*(1), 52–58.

 STRATEGY 41: Become a classroom manager before becoming a content specialist.

What the Research Says

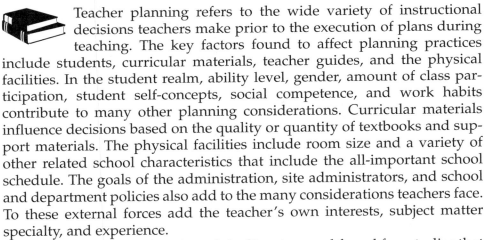 Teacher planning refers to the wide variety of instructional decisions teachers make prior to the execution of plans during teaching. The key factors found to affect planning practices include students, curricular materials, teacher guides, and the physical facilities. In the student realm, ability level, gender, amount of class participation, student self-concepts, social competence, and work habits contribute to many other planning considerations. Curricular materials influence decisions based on the quality or quantity of textbooks and support materials. The physical facilities include room size and a variety of other related school characteristics that include the all-important school schedule. The goals of the administration, site administrators, and school and department policies also add to the many considerations teachers face. To these external forces add the teacher's own interests, subject matter specialty, and experience.

Sardo-Brown (1996) reviewed the literature and found few studies that looked at novice teacher planning. Her study examined how two first-year teachers planned their first and second years of teaching and compared and contrasted the differences between the years. The two teachers in the study were selected because of their competency in their graduate education classes and because both had obtained employment in secondary schools right out of teacher education.

The most notable findings between first- and second-year planning include:

- They did not plan to emphasize content during the early weeks of school but considered management issues a higher priority.

- Both second-year novices dedicated much more time to setting up and teaching rules, procedures, and class structure along with developing early rapport with their students.

- The teachers moved further away in time and reference from their student teaching experiences where rules were routinized and planning was rule bound.

- In the second year, they were more receptive to new ideas and inservicing.

- Both planned major adjustments to their methods of assessment. Both sought out more time-efficient strategies and planned to use more high-level assessment strategies as learning devices.

- Both novices in this study married between their first and second years and looked for new ways to get more leisure time. Both credited their marriages for growing confidence in themselves as teachers and both felt "older."

- In the second year, they tried to do more of their planning at school.

- Both viewed the area of assessment as a major concern and planned numerous changes in their second year. They felt they were not prepared to successfully tackle assessment in their first year.

- Both felt more comfortable planning in their second year.

- Both continued to struggle with the problem of reconciling their own beliefs about their teaching with the incongruent beliefs of the principal and other colleagues.

- They both had a greater awareness of the cognitive and emotional needs of their students.

Application

It is clear from the research that preservice teachers move from content specialists and borrowers of instructional tactics to educators and instructional strategists their second year and thereafter. First-year teachers often don't know what they don't know until experience becomes their teacher. This is particularly true when they are faced with myriad challenges presented by students with special needs. The tactic derived from the research is to be able to learn from what teachers see in front of them rather than from what someone tells them.

Teachers should develop their own analytical skills as they implement a "best guess" instructional plan. Teachers need to do the "science" it takes to determine what happens when real students meet a teacher's management and instructional strategy. Seeing everything a teacher does as a work in progress will be comforting. Keep in mind that a teaching style is something a teacher will find in himself or herself and not something he or she learns. The classroom experience is ongoing research. Each data collection through assessment or observation tells the teacher what he or she needs to work on the following week.

Teachers will do well to also remember they are standing on the shoulders of those who came before, and they all went through similar experiences. How teachers view themselves should not be based solely on early efforts. It should be based on how teachers respond to that effort and reflection and how resilient and adaptive they can be. Analyze those problems, adjust, and move on.

Precautions and Possible Pitfalls

Don't panic! It's clear from the research that time on task is a large factor in one's development as a teacher. For most teachers, there are few shortcuts from the first days in class to the end of the year. Focusing on how students can be helped should be the priority. Teachers will gradually become less concerned with how others see them and more concerned with their students and how they learn.

Source

Sardo-Brown, D. (1996). A longitudinal study of novice secondary teachers' planning: Year two. *Teaching & Teacher Education, 12*(5), 519–530.

STRATEGY 42: *Use early literacy intervention strategies to facilitate appropriate student behavior.*

What the Research Says

After reviewing a variety of studies linking literacy delays and problem behaviors, Lane, Wehby, Menzies, Gregg, Doukas, and Muntin (2002) developed a plan to investigate the effect a phonics intervention program would have on first-grade students. The students selected for the study had been previously unsuccessful in the schoolwide literacy program as well as a social skills intervention program. The key components of this approach were that the intervention was offered during the school day and by school literacy personnel rather than the researchers themselves.

The results were dramatic, in that all of the students in the study improved their word attack skills. With the exception of one student, all of the participants exhibited a decrease in antisocial behavior on the playground and in the classroom. The implication noted by the researchers was the importance of beginning the literacy intervention as soon as possible, particularly when antisocial behavior has been noted.

Application

Often teachers make the mistake of viewing behavior problems as one issue and academic performance as another, unrelated issue. Although it is common knowledge that the frustration of a student in an academic endeavor can produce an outburst of misbehavior, there is evidence that the link is stronger than just cause and effect. Teachers can contribute to their students' success with literacy and social behavior by noticing lack of performance and offering the appropriate interventions as early as possible. Small group instruction in specific reading strategies can contribute to positive student behavior. Students who receive literacy support with phonics instruction and achieve success in reading independently seem to be calmer and better behaved in class. Whether it is the individual attention of small group instruction, the intrinsic reward of succeeding at decoding, or the actual neural connections formed in the literate brain is unclear. What is clear is the need for additional assistance for struggling students as early as possible.

Precautions and Possible Pitfalls

Caution should be taken not to assume that early literacy intervention will cure all misbehavior. Some students may have behavior disorders that need to be addressed by a psychologist. Although these students will still benefit from literacy support, phonics and reading strategy instruction may not be sufficient to meet their needs.

Source

Lane, K. L., Wehby, J. H., Menzies, H. M., Gregg, R. M., Doukas, G. L., & Muntin, S. M. (2002). Early literacy instruction for first-grade students at-risk for antisocial behavior. *Education and Treatment of Children, 25*(4), 438–459.

STRATEGY 43: If a takedown is required, restrain a student using a seated-position restraint rather than a face-down-to-the-floor restraint to reduce injury and negative psychological effects.

What the Research Says

In a British study conducted over nine months (Kaye & Allen, 2002), researchers determined that although staff in treatment centers for emotionally disturbed clients were trained in over 42 physical restraint moves, only 27 of these techniques were used. In further analysis, the researchers recommended that the training be adjusted to reflect takedown techniques that would reduce injury to clients and staff alike. In addition, the study examined the psychological effects of being restrained in a face-down position versus in a seated position. It was noted that the seated position was more socially acceptable and the potential for injury to both the client and the staff was reduced.

Application

Although it is always advisable to prevent a physical intervention by anticipating trouble, some teachers teach classes where they are asked to perform takedowns with students who require physical interventions due to emotional and behavioral issues. It is essential that these teachers be trained in the appropriate technique for that population. Teachers must ensure that any additional personnel who work with the students are also trained and understand the importance of correct restraint. The purpose of restraint is to prevent injury rather than a disciplinary measure or punishment. Keeping that in mind, the goal is to restrain the student efficiently with minimal chance for injury and minimal opportunity for further psychological distress. The seated restraint shortens the distance to travel supporting the student's weight and allows for some measure of dignity to be maintained.

Precautions and Possible Pitfalls

Teachers should never attempt to restrain a student unless they have been specifically trained to do so; the potential for injury to the teacher or the student is too great. If the teacher has not been trained and an incident arises, he or she should remove the other students from the dangerous environment as calmly and quickly as possible and notify the appropriate personnel. Most districts have specific procedures in case of an incident and usually require a written report and an IEP meeting. It is essential that teachers consider and record any antecedents to the incident as well as the student's own reflection of the incident after he or she has calmed down.

Source

Kaye, N., & Allen, D. (2002). Over the top? Reducing staff training in physical interventions. *British Journal of Learning Disabilities, 30*(3), 129–133.

5

Integrating Assistive Technology

Everyone makes mistakes. It's what you do afterward that counts.

—Anonymous

 STRATEGY 44: Ensure familiarity with available assistive technology devices that may be appropriate and beneficial for students.

What the Research Says

Bryant and Erin (1998) reviewed teacher preparation programs looking specifically for courses in assistive technology. As rapid advances are made in the field of technology, people with disabilities are making strides in accomplishing tasks that they would not have been able to accomplish before. Federal law requires that the IEP team consider the individual needs of the student specifically with regard to assistive technology. Whether the student would benefit from a low-tech device like a pencil holder or a high-tech, voice-activated word processor, the team needs to consider the available options.

A problem arises when parents and teachers are unaware of the assistive technology that is available. Although most teachers are familiar with the more obvious assistive devices that deal with physical impairments (wheelchairs, lifts, button controls, etc.), many are unaware of software advances and devices that may be more specific to a student with a particular disability. Often the insinuation is made that districts encourage teachers to avoid the topic of assistive technology in order to save money.

The main barrier to the use of assistive technology is the teacher's lack of knowledge and experience with the technology. It is of no use to have a device that the teacher cannot teach the student to operate, or a software application that is not integrated into the curriculum. Bryant and Erin (1998) cite the DLD Competencies for Teachers of Students with Learning Disabilities and suggest that a teacher preparation program include the following areas:

1. Computer literacy skills

2. General knowledge of devices and services

3. Knowledge of state and federal laws regarding assistive technology

4. Learner needs and specific devices and services that could meet those needs

5. Curricular integration and classroom environment adaptations to take advantage of the technology

6. Resources available to provide devices and funding for the technology

7. Partnerships—working with parents and other professionals to facilitate the use of technology

8. Evaluation—ability to evaluate the effectiveness of the technology and make needed adjustments

Application

Teachers need to take advantage of the training that is offered at the school site, district, or county office of education. Reading professional journals and attending conferences to keep abreast of developments in technology will help teachers be of assistance to students. Many districts have a designated assistive technology person who conducts the evaluations for the IEP team as requested. Getting to know this person and asking what kinds of things are available is a positive step.

Some teachers may be surprised to learn that the district is able to provide a laptop computer for a student with severe dysgraphia or a home lift for a student with a specific mobility need. The more comfortable the teacher is with using technology and integrating it into the curriculum, the easier it will be for the students to take advantage of the devices and services that are currently available. Whether it is something as simple as a calculator or something more complex like read-aloud computer software, it can make all the difference to a student with disabilities.

Precautions and Possible Pitfalls

Be cautious when requesting specific devices or services that don't include training for both the teacher and the student(s). When possible, teachers should attend a hands-on session that allows them to try the various applications of the device so they are comfortable when using it with their class. It is a good idea to call other teachers who are using the device with a similar population, rather than vendors, to learn the positives and negatives from an unbiased source.

Sources

Bryant, D. P., & Erin, J. (1998). Infusing a teacher preparation program in learning disabilities with assistive technology. *Journal of Learning Disabilities, 31*(1), 55–67.

Graves, A., Landers, M. F., Lokerson, J., Luchow, J., Horvath, M., & Garnett, K. (1992). *The DLD competencies for teachers of students with learning disabilities.* Reston, VA: Division for Learning Disabilities Council for Exceptional Children.

 STRATEGY 45: Spend the time needed to train students with visual impairments to use a variety of computer applications.

What the Research Says

 In a focus group study of the positive and negative aspects of computer use by people who are visually impaired or blind, researchers identified some key issues. Overwhelmingly, respondents felt that computers offered access to information and social interaction that just isn't available in other venues. Many study participants remarked on the independence granted by a computer (Gerber, 2003).

On the negative side, respondents commented on the difficulty of navigating new software applications that are Windows or menu driven, as these items are not located in the same place each time a screen is accessed (Gerber, 2003). Remember that it is not just computers that lack outside labeled buttons or switches. Many companies now produce appliances that are menu based rather than switch activated, making it very difficult for a person with visual impairments to operate independently.

Application

Many teachers are unfamiliar with the myriad software applications that are available to assist students with visual impairments. Teachers should access local resources like the Braille Institute or local SELPA (Special Education Local Plan Area that coordinates the efforts of several districts to benefit all involved) specialists to learn more about the available technology. Many of the programs available will benefit all students when used in the general education classroom. For example, software programs that read aloud what a student types can be beneficial to the emerging reader as well as to the student with visual impairments.

It is always a challenge to find the time to learn a new computer program, but the time spent in training is time recouped over the long run. Many districts will provide teachers with release time to attend training sessions. Teachers may have to seek out these opportunities, but the effort is well worth it. Additionally, time must be spent to train the student to use the assistive technology or device. It is vital that teachers ensure this time is taken and check in with students periodically to ensure that they are comfortable with the technology and are finding it helpful.

Precautions and Possible Pitfalls

Teachers should remember that there is a steep learning curve with any new software and be prepared for the inevitable frustration on the part of both student and teacher. It may seem obvious, but many manufacturers produce written manuals, which may be inaccessible to the student with visual impairments. The teacher may want to ask another student to assist with reading a help menu, or for larger segments, request a parent volunteer or a Braille Institute volunteer to read the entire manual on tape (see http://www.rfbd.org).

Source

Gerber, E. (2003). The benefits of and barriers to computer use for individuals who are visually impaired. *Journal of Visual Impairment & Blindness, 97*(9), 536–551.

STRATEGY 46: *Check periodically to ensure that assistive technology continues to be useful to students with disabilities.*

What the Research Says

In his essay in *ConnSENSE*, Edyburn (2003) calls for scrutiny of assistive technology and its efficacy with specific students. He describes a three-step process to determine if a specific device is actually serving the needs of a student with a disability. The first step is the Exploratory Phase, in which intuition and observation are employed. The second phase is the Descriptive Phase, where anecdotal and case-study information is gathered. The third phase is the Empirical Phase, where research studies, research synthesis, and meta-analysis are employed to produce statistical results.

Application

Frequently, assistive technology devices and programs are touted as highly effective with little research to prove the claim. Few people would recommend that students with disabilities be forced to wait while claims are empirically researched, and so students often become the front line of experimentation. It is essential that teachers schedule regular meetings with students to evaluate the efficacy of specific devices and ensure that they meet the students' needs. Some teachers may find that using a reflection sheet that the student or paraeducator completes is helpful to open the dialogue with the student. If the device is in use at home, the parents or other caregivers should also be included in the periodic review.

Precautions and Possible Pitfalls

Teachers must ensure that they and the students are adequately trained in the use of the specific assistive technology. Teachers should avoid the common mistake of trying to fit all the training into one session. Unless the device is very simple, it is more effective to schedule an initial training session to cover the basics, with a follow-up session a week later to answer specific questions that have arisen from practical use in the classroom.

Source

Edyburn, D. L. (2003). Assistive technology and evidence-based practice. *ConnSENSE Bulletin, 7,* 12–18.

STRATEGY 47: *Look for opportunities to increase students' communication and computer literacy skills through online assignments.*

What the Research Says

 In a study of distance learning in Australia, Frid (2001) identified some key elements to ensuring a positive learning experience for students. The course reviewed was a math exploration course aimed at students in grades 2 through 6. The environment was asynchronous and the students could choose to participate on their own timetable. Teachers adapted their role of instructional leader to facilitator of student inquiry. Most of the students were from rural communities and did not have access to trained math teachers in a face-to-face setting. The following key elements were noted:

1. Students had difficulties at first in communicating their thoughts in the e-mail format but over time developed these skills significantly.

2. Student performance was directly related to the feedback and encouragement offered by the facilitator.

Application

There is a wide range of skills and comfort levels with the use of technology in the classroom. One teacher may communicate regularly with his or her students via the Internet while the teacher next door rarely checks his or her personal e-mail. As students become more fluent in the medium, teachers need to access this avenue to increase opportunities for student learning. Teachers should encourage students to use electronic avenues to ask questions and clarify their learning. For students with disabilities, computers offer a host of support systems, including audio and visual cuing, that can enhance student understanding and participation.

To encourage this experience, teachers may first want to make use of structured computer-lab activities at the school. Students could visit a specific Web site, complete a series of tasks or answer questions, and then submit their work electronically to the teacher. Word processing skills as well as the difference between standard written English and common e-mail abbreviations should be addressed. As students increase their skills, teachers can then post assignments to the school's Web page and require the students to submit their responses electronically. As students (and teachers) continue to improve their skills, teachers may want to assign group discussion activities using a chat room, to allow students to benefit from the ideas and questions of others.

The obvious advantage to electronic support for students with disabilities is the computer programs themselves. Dictation, visual enhancement, and other assistive technology devices can greatly enhance a student's participation. A not-so-obvious advantage is the dialogue that develops between the teacher and the student outside the time constraints of the classroom. Often the greatest gift given to a student with a processing delay is the gift of time. By interacting with the student electronically in an asynchronous environment, the teacher spends the same amount of time, but the student is able to spend whatever time he or she needs to gain understanding.

Precautions and Possible Pitfalls

 Although many students now have computers in their homes, teachers should be sensitive to the fact that some may not. By taking the whole class to the school's lab or allowing students to participate using classroom computers, teachers can facilitate the acquisition of computer literacy for all students.

Source

Frid, S. (2001). Supporting primary students' on-line learning in a virtual enrichment program. *Research in Education, 11*(66), 9–28.

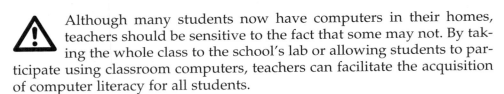

STRATEGY 48: Teach students to set goals that focus on the process of learning technology.

What the Research Says

Schunk and Ertmer (1999) studied goal setting during computer training and found that students who set process goals felt they learned more effectively than did students who set product goals. Students in the process condition believed that they were more competent in performing HyperCard tasks (i.e., they had greater self-efficacy) than did students in the product condition, and achievement results showed that process-condition students indeed were more successful than students in the product condition in performing HyperCard tasks.

It's beneficial to teach students to set learning goals for different reasons, and different kinds of goals have different effects. Goal setting can affect students' achievement and motivation, and it can affect how students regulate the use of their thoughts, actions, and feelings. Students can use the goals they set as standards for assessing their own progress. Goals focusing on the learning process emphasize the strategies that students use in acquiring skills or information. In contrast, goals focusing on the product of learning emphasize outcomes or results, such as how much was accomplished and how long it took.

Application

Have students regularly set process goals when acquiring new knowledge or skills. Use a think-aloud procedure and write on the board to model for students how they should set process goals. Individually or in groups, have students brainstorm process goals they can set for a particular computer task. Require students to write their process goals in their notebooks, and periodically check their notebooks to assess their progress in achieving their goals, looking for new goals to replace those that have already been accomplished. Some process goals may require more time than the product goals. Teachers should not underestimate the rigorous and challenging learning that technology requires when making progress toward a more primary goal or product. The following are some situations that could require as much or more time to learn than to perform the primary task. Teachers should help students make realistic time estimates and include the technology learning curve.

- Student groups needed to learn a spreadsheet and graphing program to be able to manage and summarize the data from a statistics experiment. They needed to complete a tutorial and manipulate a few small data sets before looking at their own data.

- Students using a laptop computer with a physiology (body temperature, heart rate, etc.) sensing capacity needed to learn the accompanying software to make their experiment and data collection fully functional.

- An earth science group accessing a weather and climate Web page was required to learn a Web page's specific programs to manipulate its temperature and rainfall data.

- Students from a high school located near a university needed to master the university library's online catalog to acquire the background information for their research paper.

- Students needed to evaluate many curriculum-related Internet sites to assess which sites were the most accurate and useful.

- A graphics program needed to be learned in order to develop overheads and slides to be used in an English presentation.

These are all examples of process goals that may need to be mastered before finishing a project or activity. A teacher shouldn't underestimate the potential technoprocess pitfalls and should be patient with students who may have a limited background in technology.

Precautions and Possible Pitfalls

Teachers should not just let students copy their process goals for learning to use computers or other technology. Self-generated goals are more personally meaningful to students than teacher-imposed goals.

Source

Schunk, D., & Ertmer, P. (1999). Self-regulatory processes during computer skill acquisition: Goal and self-evaluative influences. *Journal of Educational Psychology, 91*(2), 251–260.

 STRATEGY 49: Optimize the purchase and use of word processing spell checker programs to better serve the needs of students with learning disabilities.

What the Research Says

In order to facilitate a successful transition into adult life, students need to master common literacy-related skills. Coutinho, Karlan, and Montgomery (2001) and MacArthur, Graham, Haynes, and De La Paz (1996) looked at the use of spell checkers in the context of word processing. Spelling is one of those sometimes elusive yet intrinsic skills that enable individuals to communicate clearly. While many students with disabilities are able to overcome deficits in reading and math, they often retain their spelling deficits well into their adult lives. The inability to spell correctly also inhibits and limits the effective use of spelling-correction technologies. Helpful techniques such as dictionaries and personal word lists, which are commonly used to assist disabled students, can become relatively useless. Coutinho et al. and MacArthur et al. describe research that has shown that individuals with disabilities are less likely to obtain and maintain gainful employment after high school graduation. Upon graduation, students need not only vocational skills but also the literacy skills that will enable them to be competitive in the working world.

Spelling instruction, therefore, must not only include acquisition skills (remedial instruction to overcome the spelling deficit) but also compensation skills (instruction that enables the student to write with accurate spelling). Today, one popular compensation tool for writing is the word processor. Students need to become competent users of word processors and their features (e.g., spell checkers) that will enable them to compensate for spelling weaknesses. Spell checkers are able to provide target words for misspellings due to keyboarding and spelling-rule-application errors.

Unfortunately, in order for spell checkers to be a valuable tool for students with learning disabilities, the spell checker needs to provide the correct spelling for complex misspellings. According to the researchers, the spelling errors of students with learning disabilities are more complex than simple typos and rule-application errors. The misspellings can often be classified as severe phonetic mismatches, having few of the phonetic characteristics of the target word. Often spelling choices appear less mature and may contain characteristics of younger children's errors. Students with learning disabilities have also been shown to have difficulty applying spelling rules to unknown words.

With these factors in mind, Coutinho et al. (2001) and MacArthur et al. (1996) wanted to survey a range of word processing programs to identify the programs that serve the learning disabled more successfully. To accomplish this, three research questions relating to the use of spell checkers were addressed:

1. Do the various spell checkers provide the target word for misspellings first in the replacement list?

2. Do the various spell checkers generate the target word first in the replacement list equally across phonetic developmental levels?

3. Do the various spell checkers generate the target word first in the replacement list equally no matter what proportion of correct letter sequences (bigram ratio) the misspelling contains?

For this study, a search of software catalogs identified nine word processing packages that were designed for school use and included spell checkers. Two of the nine word processing programs (Write This Way and Write Outloud) were designed specifically for students with disabilities. In addition, two word processing packages commonly used in college and university settings (WordPerfect 5.2 for Windows and Microsoft Word for DOS 6.0) and two word processing programs commonly sold with computer packages (Microsoft Works 4.0 and Claris Works 4.0) were included.

Application

In creating a context for this work, it may be better to look at the problems with it first. The main problem with this study concerns the range of disabilities among students. No one program is going to be the answer for everyone. To add to the problem, this research is likely to be outdated quickly. Technology never stands still for very long. However, the research still is useful and powerful for a number of reasons. The best suggestion that comes out of this research is that spell and grammar checkers are important considerations when purchasing software, and teachers should consider their value for all student groups.

Shop for a program that best serves the needs of all students, but keep the specific requirements of the students with special needs in mind when assessing the programs. Use the information to become a better consumer of appropriate technology. It pays to consult the latest research or consumer information regarding this technology.

Precautions and Potential Pitfalls

Regardless of the software selected, it is essential that teachers build in the time it takes to become proficient in the use of the application. Take the time to become familiar with the various tools offered by the application in order to facilitate student use. It's always a good idea to contact colleagues who may be experienced with the software, and don't forget to access company help lines as needed.

Sources

Coutinho, M., Karlan, G., & Montgomery, D. (2001). The effectiveness of word processors' spell checker programs to produce target words for misspellings generated by students with learning disabilities. *Journal of Special Education Technology, 16*(2), 27–41.

MacArthur, C. A., Graham, S., Haynes, J. A., & De La Paz, S. (1996). Spelling checkers and students with learning disabilities: Performance comparisons and impact on spelling. *Journal of Special Education, 30,* 35–57.

 STRATEGY 50: Consider all aspects of technology in order to meet the accommodation needs of students with disabilities.

What the Research Says

Access to and use of electronic and information technology has the potential to promote positive postsecondary academic and career outcomes for students with disabilities. However, according to Burgstahler (2003), this potential will not be realized unless all professionals working with the disabled ensure that all individuals with disabilities have

- Equal access to technology that promotes positive academic and career outcomes
- Equal opportunities to learn to use technology in ways that contribute to positive outcomes
- Opportunities to experience a seamless transition of the availability of technology as they move through educational and career environments

Burgstahler's (2003) article is a survey and review paper examining the technological paradigm for students with disabilities. More specifically, it contrasts and compares the use of technology in both the school and employment arenas by students with and without disabilities. She found that although the benefits of technology may be even greater for people with disabilities than for people without disabilities, individuals with disabilities are less than half as likely as their nondisabled counterparts to own computers and are about one-quarter as likely to use the Internet. The design of many Web pages, instructional software programs, productivity tools, telecommunications products, and other electronic and information technologies erects barriers for some individuals with disabilities.

Burgstahler (2003) explores the role technology can play in helping students with disabilities make successful transitions to postsecondary studies, employment, and adult life. She defines terms; provides examples of electronic and information technologies and their applications in precollege and postsecondary education and employment; summarizes legal issues that apply to technology access for students with disabilities in precollege, postsecondary, and employment settings; explores promising practices; and lists topics for future research. It is important to ensure that all of the educational and employment opportunities that technology provides are accessible to everyone.

Finally, she offers an overall look at ways to level the playing field for students with disabilities and for those looking to make sense of the inherent inequalities in the way technology is used or not used by those with disabilities. According to Burgstahler (2003), barriers to technology access for individuals with disabilities include:

- A lack of trained professionals to evaluate assistive technology
- Difficulties in locating assistive technology to test by individuals with disabilities

- Confusion about existing laws and policies regarding assistive technology
- Accessible electronic and information technology
- Gaps in laws and policies that fund assistive technology
- The bureaucracy of public programs and insurance companies, particularly due to differences in laws and funding for technology between precollege and college environments

Legal mandates and accommodations for computer access for students and employees with disabilities are not always reflected in practice, even in organizations that have developed access policies. Education professionals are not always fully aware of technology options, legal issues, and appropriate strategies. These stakeholders include people with disabilities, parents, government entities, paraprofessionals, policy makers and administrators, precollege and postsecondary educators, librarians, technical support staff, and employers. Promising practices (Burgstahler, 2003) to be considered in order to reach these goals include those that follow. Most recommendations support multiple goals and serve as a trigger for reflection.

1. Administrators and policymakers should establish policies, standards, and procedures at all academic and employment levels to ensure that accessibility is considered when electronic and information technology is procured.

2. Administrators and policymakers should establish policies, standards, and procedures and provide training and support at all educational levels to ensure that Web pages, library resources, computing and science labs, and distance-learning programs are accessible to everyone, including students with disabilities.

3. Policymakers and administrators should ensure that funding is available to purchase appropriate assistive technology at all levels of academic programs, in employment settings, and during transition periods between these stages.

4. Agencies should collaborate on planning, funding, selecting, and supporting assistive technology to ensure continuous technology access and support as students with disabilities transition through academic levels and to employment.

5. Educators, librarians, parents, support staff, computer lab managers, and other stakeholders should have access to training so that they will be able to design accessible facilities and activities; select accessible computers and software; purchase appropriate assistive technology; and ensure that students with disabilities use technology for their maximum benefit as they pursue academics, careers, and self-determined lives.

6. Legislators and policymakers should take steps to clarify existing legislation; disseminate information about current laws, policies, and resources tailored to the needs of various stakeholders; and use consistent terminology and standards. They should identify and correct inconsistencies and gaps in legislation and policies regarding the selection, funding, and support of assistive technology, especially as individuals transition between all academic and employment levels.

7. Students with disabilities should be included at all stages of technology selection, support, and use so that they learn to self-advocate regarding their needs for accessible technology in the classroom and workplace.

8. Students with disabilities should be taught to use technology in ways that (1) maximize their independence, productivity, and participation in all academic and employment activities; (2) facilitate successful transitions between all academic and employment levels; and (3) lead to successful, self-determined adult lives. Technology should be used to support mentoring relationships, access to electronic information, participation in science labs, communication in class discussions, self-advocacy practice, independent living tasks, work-based learning opportunities, and other academic and career-preparation activities.

9. Students with disabilities at high school and college levels should participate in internships and other work-based learning experiences where they can practice using technology in work settings.

Application

Teachers need to ask how technology is serving the needs of students with special needs. Teachers need to become more informed advocates for appropriate technology to serve the needs of all students. If there is a problem in the ways students with disabilities interact with technology they should use the situation as an opportunity to obtain funding that may not be accessible to everyone else.

There is a role in these recommendations for everyone to consider—preservice teachers, teachers, parents, community, administrators, and policymakers. In addition, many graduates of teacher-education programs are not adequately prepared in the general use of computer technology and in classroom applications. This makes them even less qualified to help students in special education. They could benefit by becoming cognizant of these concerns. Few educational professionals give much thought to how special education students interact with technology in ways that are different from their nondisabled peers. Use this research and recommendations as a starting point for further thinking and action plans.

Precautions and Pitfalls

Technology use and choices for people with disabilities should be driven by both short-term and long-term needs, goals, and objectives. After the initial purchase, questions about who is responsible for upgrades and technical support during all life stages must be answered. Technology today quickly becomes obsolete. Funding is needed for training personnel and technical support to deliver technology services at various academic and employment levels. Teachers and students need time to acclimate and acquire technological skills as well as to increase technology awareness among all other key stakeholders, including parents, educators, librarians, service providers, employers, and people with disabilities. Planning only for the short term will lead to disappointment and a nonsustainable technological program.

Source

Burgstahler, S. (2003).The role of technology in preparing youth with disabilities for postsecondary education and employment. *The Journal of Special Education Technology, 18*(4) Retrieved December 3, 2004, from http://jset.unlv.edu/18.4/burgstahler/first.html

6

Collaborating With Colleagues and Parents

Make sure you have someone in your life from whom you can get reflective feedback.

—Warren Bennis

 STRATEGY 51: Set a positive tone for parent conferences and IEP meetings by beginning with the student's strengths.

What the Research Says

According to Rebecca K. Lytle and Judith Bordin (2001), effective IEP teams have the following characteristics: identifiable roles, positive social support, proximity, distinctiveness, fairness, similarity, and effective communication. In their article, these researchers refer to parents as "parent experts," to denote that each person present at an IEP has an equal and important role (p. 42). Parents are most familiar with the student's medical needs, likes, dislikes, and daily routine while special education and general education teachers are familiar with the academic and social needs of the student in the school setting.

Lytle and Bordin (2001) offer some suggestions for helping to create a sense of common purpose, or what they term "distinctiveness" (p. 43). By beginning the IEP meeting with a conversation about who the student is—focusing on abilities, strengths, and interests—the meeting takes on a positive tone. They recommend that the professionals present work to make the parents feel included by avoiding inside jokes and educational jargon in favor of laymen's terminology. They also warn that nonverbal communication (like eye-rolling) can be detrimental to the IEP process.

Application

 When workloads are large and teachers are busy, it can be easy to forget that the IEP process and even a parent-teacher conference intimidates many parents. Sometimes, in the effort to expedite the process, educators will zip through the formalities and rush into a presentation of the IEP without giving parents a chance to contribute. By taking a moment to establish a positive tone, the meeting can become a positive process rather than an adversarial one. This is particularly important if the student is attending the meeting along with his or her parents.

Some simple things that educators can do to contribute positively are

- Call the parent by phone to set up the meeting; inquire whether there are specific issues the parent would like to address.
- Prepare for the meeting by having teacher input, grades, assessments, etc. on hand.
- Welcome the parents with handshakes and sit next to them when possible.
- Begin the meeting with positive comments about what the student's strengths and interests are.
- Address the parents' concerns early in the meeting.
- Explain any educational jargon in laymen's terms.
- Demonstrate empathy and understanding by listening respectfully.
- Make clear notes about actions to be taken.
- End the meeting on a positive note.

Precautions and Possible Pitfalls

If teachers anticipate that a parent meeting will be adversarial, they should enlist the support of a professional who is a skilled facilitator. Many administrators and counselors have specific training in conflict mediation. He or she will guide the discussion to a positive exchange while preventing participants from overstepping appropriate boundaries. It is always possible to postpone a meeting in a respectful manner if tension is high and the chances of a productive outcome are slim.

Source

Lytle, R. K., & Bordin, J. (2001). Enhancing the IEP team. *Teaching Exceptional Children, 33*(5), 40–45.

 STRATEGY 52: Take the time to discuss everyday examples of teaming issues before they arise in the classroom.

What the Research Says

 Schamber (1999) discusses aspects of everyday teaming relationships that can ultimately undermine the collaborative efforts of the teachers involved:

- Support fellow team members: Schamber (1999) warns that although a supportive relationship is a common side effect of the teaming arrangement, teachers should be careful not to overstep the bounds of that support.
- Discuss team concerns without all team members present: This erodes trust among members.
- Speak on behalf of a team member who is not present: Although it may be convenient, absent team members may feel overlooked or misrepresented.
- Assist with classroom discipline: Any action or advice should be offered constructively to avoid feelings of criticism, particularly in front of students.

Application

As soon as teachers know that they will be teaming with another professional, they need to schedule time for the team to get together to discuss the process before they begin working with students. Although the temptation is often to move right into curricular planning, it is vital that the team discuss the more practical aspects of what it means to work together. Often a good way to open this conversation is simply with a description of what an effective learning environment looks like versus what an ineffective learning environment looks like. By comparing notes on these two scenarios, team members can begin to discern the kinds of things that are important to them (classroom rules, desk arrangement, noise level, etc.). Following this, a discussion of work habits and pet peeves can also facilitate understanding. It is not necessary for team members to have the same opinions, but an equitable agreement should be reached prior to students arriving. Once the management issues have been discussed, the team can move on to curricular planning for their specific students.

Precautions and Possible Pitfalls

 Although flexibility is a key component of a positive teaming relationship, team members shouldn't hesitate to address issues soon after they arise—letting them build up is neither professional nor effective in the long run. If necessary, asking a trusted outsider (department chair, administrator) to help guide the team through the discussion process may be appropriate.

Source

Schamber, S. (1999). Surviving team teaching's good intentions. *Education Digest, 64*(8), 18–24.

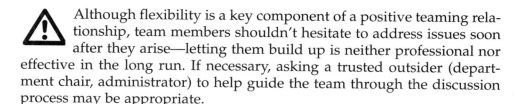

STRATEGY 53: *Ensure that time is built into the workday to communicate with the paraeducator.*

What the Research Says

 Riggs and Lock (2001) identified 20 recommendations for working with paraeducators effectively. Most prominently, they emphasize the importance of communication. Not only do they advise that paraeducators have a specific written job description but that they should be included in the team meeting that determines their role in the inclusive classroom. It is vital that paraeducators be familiar with district rules and polices, but even more important is their understanding of the specific needs of the individual students they are working with.

Exemplary districts provide training for paraeducators and provide opportunities for ongoing communication between teacher and paraeducator outside of the classroom. Riggs and Lock (2001) also noted the importance of demonstrating respect for paraeducators by providing desks and work areas as well as valuing their input.

Application

Paraeducators are an important resource in the inclusion process, often making the difference in a child's successful academic placement. One of the most important facets of a paraeducator's job is to communicate with individual teachers. Few districts have the resources to employ paraeducators on a full-time basis, and so it is common to have paraeducators who work partial shifts that begin or end inside school hours. With all the duties teachers have, it can be an impossible feat to find time to effectively communicate with a paraeducator. When possible, teachers should locate a break time during which they and the paraeducator can meet to discuss particular students' progress and any other issues that may have arisen. Failing that, some teachers use a journal that can be passed back and forth to document questions, concerns, or other information that will facilitate efficacy on both sides.

Precautions and Possible Pitfalls

Often paraeducators are hired and placed within such a short time that no training is offered. Teachers should be cautious to avoid skipping this vital step due to circumstances. It is a more effective use of resources to pay for a substitute or overtime hours in order to ensure that a paraeducator has the training he or she requires in order to fully understand the needs of the individual students he or she will be working with as well as district policies and procedures. Teachers may need to coordinate with district administrators to accomplish this.

Source

Riggs, C. G., & Lock, R. H. (2001). Work effectively with paraeducators in inclusive settings. *Intervention in School & Clinic, 37*(2), 114–118.

 STRATEGY 54: *Take the time to "meet parents where they are" to form meaningful parent-school partnerships.*

What the Research Says

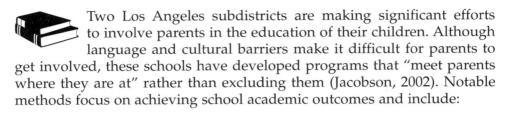 Two Los Angeles subdistricts are making significant efforts to involve parents in the education of their children. Although language and cultural barriers make it difficult for parents to get involved, these schools have developed programs that "meet parents where they are at" rather than excluding them (Jacobson, 2002). Notable methods focus on achieving school academic outcomes and include:

- Interactive homework sessions in which teachers teach parents and students key concepts
- Math Nights and Open Court Nights focusing on family learning
- Learning Walks where parents visit classrooms during the school day
- Computer Literacy and Immigration classes for parents
- Mother-Daughter College Prep where mothers learn how to prepare their daughters to be the first generation to attend college
- Tea for 10 where parents of successful students share their methods
- Cross-mentoring where parents of struggling students mentor other students who are having trouble while another parent mentors their child

Application

Most parents want to have a positive relationship with their children and many have a strong desire to help their children succeed at school. However, many parents also feel uncomfortable with their abilities when it comes to offering academic support—particularly at the secondary level. By taking the time to understand the culture and experience of the specific parents at their school, teachers can determine the best program to meet parents' abilities and needs. The first steps should be to conduct an informal assessment of the situation. Small, single-meeting activities will often yield more positive results than weekly events, until parents become more comfortable attending. Schools should consider offering a joint parent-student homework support session focusing on a single academic subject or specific project. Some teachers may be more comfortable establishing a Web site where parents can check student grades and course assignments. Finding the right level of involvement for parents and teachers is an individual and ongoing process.

Precautions and Possible Pitfalls

Don't make the mistake of evaluating a program or event on the basis of the number of parents who attend. People lead very busy lives and are often unable to follow through with all the things they would like to. In addition, some cultures view teachers as the ultimate authority and do not question what the school does. In these cases, lack of attendance should not be misinterpreted as lack of support. Any effort teachers make to involve students' parents in their education will have a positive effect.

Source

Jacobson, L. (2002). Putting the "parent piece" in schools. *Education Week, 22*(5), 1–4.

 STRATEGY 55: *Consider consulting with the speech pathologist to create a multifaceted approach to build students' vocabulary and assist them in reading comprehension.*

What the Research Says

Johnson, Tulbert, Sebastian, Devries, and Gompert (2000) describe an inclusive classroom model where the speech pathologist, special education teacher, and general education teacher collaborate on lesson planning and delivery for a vocabulary unit. Using a language-board approach, the three teachers selected the words that their fifth-grade students would need to comprehend a specific story, taking into account the specific goals of the students receiving special services.

The result was a vocabulary lesson that included the following instructional approaches:

1. Mnemonic keyword—structuring a similar sounding word to key into the original word

2. Interactive Process—students design their own memory clues and images about a word

3. Rehearsal—students hear the definition of a word and then repeat it

4. Holistic instruction—students learn about syntax, morphology, semantics, and pragmatics for a given word

5. Paired oral and written language—students use the words (reading, writing, listening, and speaking)

Application

Students demonstrate a wide range of vocabulary development in any classroom, but even more so when they have learning disabilities. Issues with auditory processing and short- and long-term memory can adversely affect their reading comprehension. Many teachers will prepare students for unfamiliar vocabulary with a word list and definitions. Although this technique is popular and many textbooks include word lists, students aren't always able to internalize these words to the level where they aid comprehension—particularly in other contexts.

Using the services of a speech pathologist can assist teachers in developing a multifaceted approach to vocabulary instruction. Understanding word origins and morphology can assist students in their long-range understanding of language as well as give them the tools they need to decode unfamiliar words. By combining this approach with student-created mnemonics as well as formal definitions, students demonstrate increased comprehension.

Precautions and Possible Pitfalls

Teachers need to be wary of requiring students to learn long lists of vocabulary out of context. Although students may be able to recall these words for tests, the meanings are quickly lost when the words are not in the context of reading or writing.

Source

Johnston, S. S., Tulbert, B. L., Sebastian, J. P., Devries, K., & Gompert, A. (2000). Vocabulary development: A collaborative effort for teaching content. *Intervention in School & Clinic, 35*(5), 311–316.

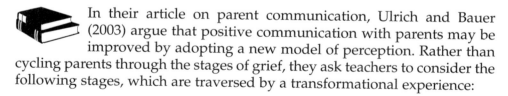

STRATEGY 56: Consider the level or stage parents are at regarding their child with a disability before recommending specific services and accommodations.

What the Research Says

In their article on parent communication, Ulrich and Bauer (2003) argue that positive communication with parents may be improved by adopting a new model of perception. Rather than cycling parents through the stages of grief, they ask teachers to consider the following stages, which are traversed by a transformational experience:

1. The Ostrich Phase—often confused with denial, this may be a state of lack of information

2. Special Designation—the parent accepts that the child has a disability and is now actively (sometimes aggressively) seeking help for the child

3. Normalization—the parent seeks to find normal, peer-appropriate activities for the child

4. Self-Actualization—recognition that the child needs supports, and dreams are replaced with realities as the child learns to self-advocate

Ulrich and Bauer (2003) encourage teachers to use the stages and determine what level a parent is at to help the communication process. One day a parent might request a one-on-one aide (level 2) and then contradict that statement by asking for the child to be placed in the general education classroom (level 3). Rather than be frustrated by this turnaround, teachers would be wise to understand that a transformational moment has occurred, allowing the parent to move to the next level.

Application

It is important that teachers and parents communicate effectively prior to making decisions that affect students. An important part of this process is recognizing where each party is coming from and truly understanding what his or her vision is for the student. Teachers can facilitate this communication by asking questions that link to the levels identified by Ulrich and Bauer (2003). By questioning parents about types of services and listening to their responses, teachers can explore what level a parent is at. For instance, asking if the child knows about his or her disability can often indicate parent level. Although the teacher may be ready to assist the student with self-advocacy skills, parents may still need the reassurance that there is a safety net, in the form of teacher follow-up, available for the student.

Precautions and Possible Pitfalls

The greatest danger in parent communication is assuming that the teacher knows better than the parent. Teachers should always take the time to ask and offer choices to ensure that they are on the right track and shouldn't forget to include the student if he or she is able to speak about his or her preferences. Teachers might ask, "I know you would like weekly updates on Mary's progress. Would you feel more comfortable e-mailing her teachers? Or, we have a form she can have her teachers sign as she attends class." In addition, although identifying stages may help a teacher gain insight, parents are individuals and should be treated individually.

Source

Ulrich, M. E., & Bauer, A. M. (2003). Levels of awareness. *Teaching Exceptional Children, 35*(6), 20–25.

 STRATEGY 57: Spend the time it takes to ensure a positive team-teaching experience.

What the Research Says

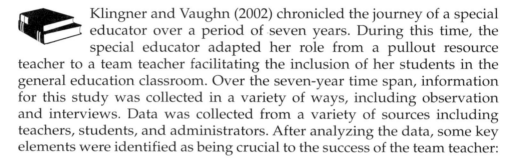 Klingner and Vaughn (2002) chronicled the journey of a special educator over a period of seven years. During this time, the special educator adapted her role from a pullout resource teacher to a team teacher facilitating the inclusion of her students in the general education classroom. Over the seven-year time span, information for this study was collected in a variety of ways, including observation and interviews. Data was collected from a variety of sources including teachers, students, and administrators. After analyzing the data, some key elements were identified as being crucial to the success of the team teacher:

1. Interpersonal communication skills

2. Knowledge of the curriculum in order to provide adaptations or alternative assignments

3. Knowledge of the individual students' abilities, disabilities, and IEPs

4. Personal flexibility and creativity

Application

Working with another professional in a classroom where the teacher has been used to autonomy can be a challenge for even the most dedicated teacher. As more and more schools move to an inclusion model relying on team teachers to deliver needed services to students with disabilities in the general education classroom, it is essential that the team teachers take the time to ensure positive ongoing communication.

Ideally, the team teachers will meet and plan their lessons prior to the start of school. The required curriculum should be considered along with the specific needs of the students enrolled in the class. Specific students' IEP goals should be noted and any accommodation or modifications identified and accounted for in the lesson design. Additionally, teachers will benefit from having an open and frank discussion about the classroom environment and discipline policy.

As the team begins their instruction with the students, they should continue to communicate about positive experiences and areas for improvement. Often teachers who were reluctant to team teach at first will find they enjoy the camaraderie and feedback available from their team teachers. Team teachers often find that they gradually fall into patterns that enhance instruction and provide maximum support for students with special needs. The consistent reflection that successful teams engage in helps foster the flexibility that is essential for successful teaming.

Precautions and Possible Pitfalls

 Sometimes well-meaning administrators will team two teachers together in order to offer support to a weaker teacher. This practice is inappropriate and unfair to both teachers. The weaker teacher needs training and administrative support to improve his or her skills rather than having the issue swept under the carpet. The stronger teacher needs a team partner who is skilled and effective to create the most positive experience for the students.

Source

Klingner, J. K., & Vaughn, S. (2002). The changing roles and responsibilities of an LD specialist. *Learning Disability Quarterly, 25*(1), 19–32.

 STRATEGY 58: Consider how parents might be reacting to their child with a learning disability and how that might affect the student in class.

What the Research Says

 Ferguson and Asch (1989) reviewed the research on family reactions to having a child with a disability. From this review and investigation, they developed a conceptual framework to locate the major research orientations that developed over the last century. Ferguson (2002) found two new strands that have emerged in more recent research, and his review explores how these approaches promise more useful interpretive frames for efforts to improve linkages between families and schools.

As with many social phenomena, a family's interpretation of the meaning of disability cannot help but reflect to some degree the larger context of social attitudes and historical realities within which that interpretation emerges. Ferguson and Asch (1989) tried to reflect the interpretations of families within the research orientations of the time. They state this shared activity between researchers and parents is "meaning-making" that ties us to our current time and place. They characterize their work as a snapshot of what interpretations seem to fit best right now and a review of how these current interpretations have evolved over time.

The challenge was to catalog and sequence the evidence of parental damage and to argue for the efficacy of this or that therapeutic intervention. The basic two questions they looked at were

1. What is the nature of parental reaction to having a child with a disability?

2. What is the source of this reaction?

Ferguson (2002) dealt with how the answers to these questions have changed over time. Today, there is no longer an emphasis on how poor and probably disabled parents breed poor and inevitably disabled children. Professionals have shifted their attention to how children with disabilities inevitably damage the families into which they are born. Whether they preferred to use primarily attitudinal (guilt, denial, displaced anger, grief) categories or behavioral ones (role disruption, marital cohesiveness, social withdrawal), most researchers assumed a connection that was both intrinsic and harmful. They go on to describe and characterize a range of repeated responses typical of families. The main points of their interest are the following:

- Psychodynamic Approach: The Neurotic Parent
- Functionalist Approach: The Dysfunctional Parent
- Interactionist Approach: The Powerless Parent
- Psychosocial Approach: The Suffering Parent
- The Adaptive Family
- The Supported Family (Ferguson, 2002, pp. 125–128)

Application

First keep in mind that the term "family" can describe and categorize a wide range of living conditions for a student, and relationships to family may have drastically changed over time for a child. Consider how an identified disability has "damaged" the parents and family and how the family and the student have responded or reacted to the "damage." Much of the time, a disability is seen as a message telling the parents what the student can't do or what he or she can't become in his or her life. Also, many times it's the child's teachers who bring the messages. This can put teachers in a less-than-favorable role.

Teachers are part of a team of adults concerned about the individual students in their classes. Regardless of where one comes down on the cultural and societal context of families and children with disabilities, there are an immense variety of beliefs and practices that have an undeniably powerful influence on how a specific family interprets a specific disability.

Teachers will often be pulled into this mix, and it is a good idea to have some understanding of the potential structure of the situation and how they might choose to react ahead of time.

According to the research, parents may present or prefer to use primarily attitudinal (guilt, denial, displaced anger, grief) categories or behavioral ones (role disruption, marital cohesiveness, social withdrawal) as a reaction to the disability. They might be apathetic or involved, angry or accepting. They might express displeasure with support providers over a supposed lack of supports, as displaced anger originally directed at the child. Teachers may want to examine their own performance inadequacies before categorizing the parental response as nonjustifiable anger toward the system.

On the positive side, Ferguson and Asch (1989) found there is increasing recognition that many families cope effectively and positively with the additional demands experienced in parenting a child with a disability. They found in the most recent literature that families of children with disabilities exhibit variability comparable to the general population with respect to important outcomes.

Some suggestions for general education teachers are:

1. Read IEPs. There is nothing less professional than not being familiar with students' issues or their performance in class.

2. Be prepared to deal with parents who exhibit many of the characteristics described here. Check with special education teachers or counselors who may have been dealing with the parents before making contact.

3. Discuss strategies for contact with counselors and special education teachers.

4. Be prepared to focus on what is best for the child. Avoid discussing curricular or instructional needs and constraints.

5. Remember to avoid telling parents what their child can't do. Keep hope alive with positive comments and strategies well thought out before contacting parents.

6. Listen carefully, as parents may provide information that will help.

Precautions and Possible Pitfalls

 Always put the needs of the students first. Put coverage or keeping up teacher needs on the back burner. Much of the time student needs and curricular needs are not the same. Most importantly, parents are not concerned with anything but their children and how the teacher can help them.

Sources

Ferguson, P. M. (2002). A place in the family: An historical interpretation of research on parental reactions to having a child with a disability. *Journal of Special Education, 36*(3), 124–131.

Ferguson, P. M., & Asch, A. (1989). Lessons from life: Personal and parental perspectives on school, childhood, and disability. In D. P. Biklen, D. L. Ferguson, & A. Ford (Eds.), *Schooling and disability: Eighty-eighth yearbook of the National Society for the Study of Education, Part II* (pp. 108–140). Chicago: National Society for the Study of Education.

 STRATEGY 59: Reduce the number of special education referrals by educating general education teachers about the referral process, including what to look for and how to teach using a variety of approaches.

What the Research Says

 In a study of 63 teachers at a variety of school sites, Drame (2002) found that teachers were more likely to refer students for special educational assessment when:

- Instructional approach of the teacher included more whole-group delivery than small-group activities mixed with direct instruction
- A prereferral process was not in place at the school
- The specific class was predominantly lower socioeconomically and the school size was over 2,000 students
- A larger number of students in the class were disruptive

Application

 Schools should establish a clear and practical referral process at each site. Schools should have a quick reference sheet that outlines what the process is and who is responsible for each step. Special educators should take the opportunity in staff meetings or on inservice days to specifically address the referral process with general education teachers to ensure that they are familiar with the steps involved.

When possible, inservices should include some practical advice regarding what types of behaviors (both academic and social) could be indicators of a student with special needs. Often it is helpful if general education teachers understand how students qualify for special education services by demonstrating a significant discrepancy between their ability and performance as a result of a specific learning disability. Sometimes teachers believe that a student who is not as capable automatically qualifies for special education.

It is also a good idea to remind teachers about learning styles and multiple intelligences. Although many are familiar with these ideas, most teachers tend to teach the way they were taught unless they actively choose to approach instruction differently.

It is important to ensure there is follow-up with the referring teachers to let them know the result of the referral. Often teachers never hear back what a team has decided. Teachers benefit from hearing that their referral produced a positive action to help a student succeed.

Precautions and Possible Pitfalls

 Some teachers make the majority of the referrals. It is a good idea to check the results of these referrals to see if the teacher has an uncanny eye for spotting students in need or if he or she would benefit from some support in discriminating between problems of attitude versus problems of disability.

Source

Drame, E. R. (2002). Sociocultural context effects on teachers' readiness to refer for learning disabilities. *Exceptional Children, 69*(1), 41–54.

 STRATEGY 60: Consider coteaching and collaboration to meet the needs of students with disabilities.

What the Research Says

Most teachers realize the benefits of collaborating with colleagues to problem solve and troubleshoot. In today's classrooms, the challenges teachers face in trying to meet the educational, social, and emotional needs of diverse learners can be overwhelming. Teacher educators are increasingly realizing the benefits of teamwork. With school reform and restructuring, and the "least restrictive environment" practice taking the spotlight, coplanning and coteaching may provide powerful ways to address the demands of students with special needs (Hafernick, Messerschmitt, & Vandrick, 1997). Many schools are now using the model of coteaching for their special needs population. In this model, the general education and special education teachers coteach in the same classrooms.

In a 1999 study by Duchardt, Marlow, Inman, Christensen, and Reeves, the special education faculty of a university in Louisiana initiated collaborative opportunities with the general education faculty for coplanning and coteaching. Teachers met once a week, over lunch, to discuss course content and lesson delivery. As an outgrowth of these meetings, meeting participants developed a coplanning and coteaching model to assist other educators who wished to collaborate. A step-by-step design of this model follows.

Stage 1. Choose a trusted teacher with whom to collaborate. Obstacles can result when misunderstandings or miscommunications occur. The goal of collaboration is clear: success for special education students. The more this goal is discussed and used as a motivating factor, the more trust can be established and the greater the rapport that is generated.

Stage 2. Find pockets of time to plan. Carve out small blocks of time in the beginning to meet with other team members to discuss course content. Down the road, planning can occur on an as-needed basis, or even by phone or e-mail.

Stage 3. Brainstorm! After discussing course content, team members can brainstorm options for coteaching the lesson. Brainstorming helps establish the expertise of each team member and permits planning to advance easily and without delay.

Stage 4. Prepare the actual lesson. The team members discuss, prepare, and develop a written guide for coteaching the lesson. Consider having the lesson videotaped to assess and amend the lesson plan for future use.

Stage 5. Coteach the lesson. The first time a lesson is cotaught, the two teachers must test the new instructional strategies. At this point, the preparation time will be obvious in its value. Until the lesson is taught, the teachers will have no idea whether the first four strategies are working or whether additional strategies for coteaching will be needed. Once the lesson is done, the teachers can evaluate its success.

Stage 6. Support your team members. A necessary skill for the effective teacher to possess is the capability to be flexible and add to or emphasize key points throughout the lesson. Each team member needs to establish a comfortable and secure working relationship as well as trust in the intentions of the other team members.

Stage 7. Assess the lesson. After the lesson is presented, each team member can provide the presenting teacher with feedback. If the lesson was videotaped, team members can view the ways in which the lesson can be improved or polished. Having other trusted colleagues view the lesson might also provide valuable insights.

According to the study by Duchardt et al. (1999), coplanning and coteaching arrangements can result in nine positive outcomes:

1. Collaboration and development of trust

2. Learning to be flexible and collegial

3. Finding pockets of time to coplan

4. Learning through trial and error

5. Forming teaching and learning partnerships

6. Challenging ourselves and developing professionally

7. Solving problems as a team

8. Meeting the needs of diverse learners

9. Meeting the needs of teachers as problem solvers (pp. 189–190)

Application

The African proverb "It takes a village to raise a child" can be adapted in education today to read, "It takes a whole school to educate a child." With the needs of special education students and other diverse learners, coplanning and coteaching offer students (and teachers) opportunities for success. The collaboration between general education teachers, special education teachers, school counselors, speech therapists, and other school professionals can make a critical difference in helping students with special needs achieve.

Precautions and Possible Pitfalls

While more and more schools are using a team approach when dealing with special needs students, caution should be taken. Team members must be committed to making this model work. Each member of the team provides expertise and insights critical to the success of students involved. Also, general education teachers sometimes aren't used to team teaching and may feel uncomfortable having another teacher in their classrooms. Coteaching should be just that. The special education teacher should not become an aide for the general education teacher but an integral part of the lesson. This is where planning is of critical importance.

Sources

Duchardt, B., Marlow, L., Inman, D., Christensen, P., & Reeves, M. (1999). Collaboration and co-teaching: General and special education faculty. *Clearing House, 72*(3) (Special Section: Culture and the Schools), 186–191.

Hafernick, J. J., Messerschmitt, D. S., & Vandrick, S. (1997). Collaborative research: Why and how? *Educational Researcher, 26*(9), 31–35.

Afterword

Helping Special Learners
Succeed in Inclusive Classrooms

Fifty years ago, special education as we know it today didn't exist and students who fell outside the "average" range were enrolled in special schools, institutions, or simply kept at home. We've come a long way and we are proud of our progress, but more research still needs to be conducted and new findings need to be incorporated into the way we teach all students.

Universal Design for Instruction is a worthy goal. The idea of teachers considering all students and their individual needs before designing instruction and assessment practices has been a long time coming. What a difference this approach makes to teachers who no longer have to adjust and adapt their lessons and assessments to accommodate students because the needed flexibility is already built in. But most significantly, what a difference for each student who can come to school ready to learn knowing that his or her needs can be met!

Ultimately, all teachers are researchers, and we conduct daily studies into what is effective in our own classrooms with our own students. And while we may not always publish our findings, it is our professional obligation to share our "research" with our colleagues while learning from their "research" as well. It is our own ongoing learning that promotes the ongoing learning of our students. Life-long learning isn't just a catch phrase; it is the hallmark of excellence as we continue to work on our practice.

Formal research is readily available through journals and other publications in hard copy and online. With the demands of legislation like NCLB requiring research-based teaching practices, today more than ever teachers need to keep abreast of changes in the field. Good teachers know what works—they've discovered that through trial and error with a good measure of experience. Our intention with this book was to cut down on some of the time involved in locating and analyzing the research, allowing our readers to skip ahead to the part where research makes a difference in the lives of students. We hope that we've accomplished that goal.

Index

CORWIN PRESS

The Corwin Press logo—a raven striding across an open book—represents the union of courage and learning. Corwin Press is committed to improving education for all learners by publishing books and other professional development resources for those serving the field of K–12 education. By providing practical, hands-on materials, Corwin Press continues to carry out the promise of its motto: **"Helping Educators Do Their Work Better."**